"It isn't enough to talk about peace. One must believe in it. And it isn't enough to believe in it. One must work at it."

Eleanor Roosevelt

"Music is the language of the spirit. It opens the secret of life, bringing peace, abolishing strife."

Khalil Gibran

"If we have no peace, it is because we have forgotten we belong to each other."

Mother Teresa

Dec. 2011

May Peace Be
Be with you
now and forever —

Lefe.

WHAT IS PEACE?
MESSAGES FROM THE HEART

LEXIE BROCKWAY POTAMKIN
ORIGINAL ART FROM PAINTINGS BY ANATOLY IVANOV

Library of Congress Cataloging-in Publication Data

What Is Peace? Messages From The Heart / [compiled by] Lexie Brockway Potamkin; artwork by Anatoly Ivanov.

ISBN   978-0-9824590-0-3 (hardcover)

First Printing, October, 2009

Printed in Malaysia by Palace Press International

I dedicate this book to Alura "Laura,"
who taught me everything!

"My religion is very simple – my religion is kindness."

Dalai Lama

Acknowledgments

What is Peace? Inevitably, peace starts from within, within the hearts and minds of our world leaders, within our classrooms, within our corporations, institutions, and ultimately, within ourselves.

Just as peace is a collaborative process, this book on peace would not have been possible without the participation of so many wonderful people from all over the world who generously share their own thoughts about peace. their contributions are remarkable. We are truly blessed to receive them.

My gratitude to Anatoly Ivanov, whose exquisitely beautiful artwork inspires peace and grace. A special thank you to Elliott Curson, dear friend and colleague. Without his steadfast support, this book would never have been completed. My appreciation and thanks to Juan Guerrero, loyal and dedicated co-worker, who tirelessly and meticulously compiled the peace responses. To Gregg Anderson, my appreciation of his infinitely expansive mind and open heart.

And I am deeply grateful to my family and close friends. Their unconditional love keeps me going.

CONTENTS

Introduction

The real and lasting victories are those of peace, and not of war.
Ralph Waldo Emerson

Have you ever watched a hawk or an eagle catch waves of air and soar? When I sit by the ocean, or next to a river, I feel peace. We've all experienced the feeling of peace in our lives, but far too often those moments are fleeting. We lead busy lives. Consciously or sub-consciously, we long for more peace in our hectic lives. Meditation makes me more peaceful. Often, after I meditate, I'll return to my busy life with husband, children, and pets with a new sense of awareness.

I believe "No" is as sacred as "Yes." Sometimes I have to say no when I'm pulled in a dozen directions, to find a more solid sense of well-being. I learn more and more each day about peace from within, and how to achieve it. I find inner peace deep within my heart.

When are you at peace? Do you fall into it, or come to it by practice, or education? Can you find peace in a song? Does a kitten's purr render peace, or birdsong, or the fragrance of a garden after it rains? What is your peace?

When I wrote my first book, *What Is Spirit?* I subtitled it *Messages from the Heart.* I can't answer the question "What Is Spirit?" from a logical mind. It must be answered from the heart. "What Is Peace?" is a heart question, too.

Kenosis is Greek for "letting go," the opposite of clinging. I believe inner peace is found somewhere within the journey of letting go.

My father was a peaceful man. He was easygoing and his unconditional love for our family and friends was a powerful example for my brother, my sister and me. My dad was an engineer. He took jobs as employers needed him around the country, so when I was growing up we moved every few years. My dad didn't cling to places or material things. He was calm, gentle, and forgiving. Although, as children, my brother, sister and I were disciplined, Dad let go of past transgressions. Always. He didn't judge anyone by the color of their skin, their gender, or their job. Ultimately, he got cancer and had to let go of his glorious life at age 57.

I now understand that almost everything I learned about peace, consciousness, spirit, and love, I drew from my parents, Mickey and Laura. Those who knew them felt they were enlightened souls. Growing up, I heard over and over, "Your parents are so loving and warm." Hugging, in our family, was a big deal. I recall when my husband first met my Aunt Karen. She threw her arms around him, and he stood there, frozen. A stranger had hugged him. A stranger!

We weren't a perfect family. Like everyone, we had struggles concerning jobs, money, moving, and all the things you acquire and deal with over the years. After we argued we would say we were sorry. We'd forgive one another, and move on. When my father took another job somewhere on the other side of the country, I had to leave friends behind, create new relationships, deal with unfamiliar climates, geography, and highways. My family kept me strong. We stuck together. Those experiences made me resilient. Learning to let go is a process based on flexibility.

Although my parents didn't have fancy titles and PhDs, they taught us to live life with love, compassion, and forgiveness. They didn't preach, but lived it. Some refer to this as walking the walk, or making your life the argument. My dad used to say, "It's more important to be loving than to be right." He was never too busy to hug or ask how our day was. I was so attracted to his kind, peaceful energy, that I followed him around, everywhere, just to be in his presence. He uplifted my spirit. When he was busy working or talking with others, there I was, hopping or leaping around him like a frog. Hence, my nickname, "Toad." And the early admiration I held for my dad has stayed with me my whole life.

What was it about Jesus, Moses, Buddha, Gandhi, or any enlightened being that attracts people? Perhaps, like Albert Schweitzer, they all experience a peaceful reverence for life. What was it about my father Mickey that we felt such love in his presence? My dad used to say, "Righteousness is just ego. Love is all that matters." I could be in a lousy mood, upset and angry, but the moment

I saw my dad, I felt better, and more serene because of *his* serenity. How did he maintain it? I never had the chance to ask him. My dad was the youngest of twelve. When I asked his brothers and sisters how he became so kind, they all said the same thing: He was born that way.

My mother hung a plaque in our house that read: "Love works in ways that are wondrous and strange, and there's nothing in life that love cannot change." I would ask her if love could change a mean girl at school, or if love could change how lonely I felt when we moved to a new city every few years. Her answer was always the same: Yes! Yes!

Now I know this is true. I believe in the miracle of love, that pure mystical intimacy with the mercy of God. My mother, during her lifetime, lost a son, and her husband and soul-mate. She endured four open-heart surgeries, and came through each operation with gratitude and a loving, warm smile. When I was a child and friends came over to play, my mother would meet them at the door with a smile. She would say, "Welcome to our home! I'm so happy you're here!" If anybody ever walked in angry, they didn't stay that way.

The Hebrew word *Shalom*, used to greet people and to say good-bye, literally means "peace." It's linked to another word, *Shalem*, meaning "whole again," which leads back to the basis of Jewish belief, the oneness of God, and the peace within. Although my mother was Christian, she could have spoken her words of welcome in any language, and in any tradition. Upon entering her loving home, one would know the oneness of God, and the peace within.

I witnessed my mom expanding her love and consciousness, especially during the last years of her life. She learned to let go of the small frustrations in life. If she lost her car keys, for example, she'd laugh about it, and make a joke about her memory. She was so adventurous she'd try almost anything: scuba diving, wave runners, horseback riding. She loved to travel to Venice, her favorite city. She learned how to email in her eighties. She moved to a new condominium, mastered new dances, made new friends, and attended personal growth workshops. She let cars pass ahead of her, and would say, "I don't want to miss an opportunity to be kind."

In the months before she died, she would say, "Let me go to sleep alone tonight, so I can talk to God." Half an hour before she passed away, I was at her side. She was in a coma, but suddenly opened her eyes and whispered, "I love you." Then, she let go of her earthly life and evolved into the next realm. She became a guide and a light force to me and my family.

"Be careful how you live, you may be the only Bible some people will ever read" -- this was a favorite saying of my parents. I didn't have to read the Bible – my parents were examples of how to live. I don't know how they knew these things, but I am grateful they did. I'm an orphan now, and yet the wisdom of my parents never leaves me.

Although I've always considered myself spiritual, what does that mean? I've felt deep, profound peace when I meditate and chant with Tibetan Buddhist monks. I feel serene when I'm practicing a centering prayer. I have learned to tap into a deep, universal, unconditional love always there to support me. At times I feel a peaceful undertow, almost like a calming river flowing through me, even when my outside world is chaotic and stressful. Losing my parents was everything tragic. *So I thought.*

I believe Divine intervention plays a major role in our lives, and gives us opportunities to learn. What is Divine intervention? When my dad died, I was 19. I questioned life and its purpose, the harshness of death, and the existence of an afterlife. I began to soul-search on a spiritual path.

Nearly 30 years after Dad died, my mother passed away. I had a husband and three small children. My mother had been my best friend and wisdom teacher. When she died, I felt spiritually alone, and abandoned. During this sad, depressing time, the universe provided me with another advisor and wisdom teacher, Reverend Cynthia Bourgeault. Through her teachings, I began to heal. Then, last December, there was another loss. In my twenties and thirties I spent 15 years building a company. I invested most of my savings with Bernie Madoff. I put complete trust in him. Investors like me thought our money was safe and solid. Madoff stole billions of dollars from thousands of people.

Many lost everything as a result of his crimes: homes and businesses, even philanthropic organizations. Gone. In a snap. All gone. As for my family, at least we still have our home, our health, and the ability to pay our bills. We're fortunate. Others will never recover. I was stunned, angry, and grief-stricken, not only for my loss, but for those friends of mine, even those I didn't know, who were victims of Bernie Madoff.

Loss of loved ones, loss of material possessions — these events can be an opportunity for rebirth. We have to "die" and let go of our old selves in order to truly live and find peace. Through Cynthia Bourgeault's teachings, in meditation and visualization, and with the wisdom the Spiritual Paths Institute provided, I was able, in time, to move to a deeper place where I felt forgiveness, peace, and a state of grace.

Along with Cynthia Bourgeault, other teachers at the Spiritual Paths Institute guided me: Rabbi Rami Shapiro, PhD; Kabir and Camille Helminski; Swami Amarupananda, Vajaprana, and Edward Bastian, PhD. I studied the deepest, most mystical, loving aspects of five spiritual traditions. All tapped into unconditional love. I asked myself daily: Can I be more kind, generous, forgiving, and tolerant? I learned my own personal peace could become peace for others.

At the time I lost my savings, I found myself synchronously reclaiming my Christian roots. I read Cynthia Bourgeault's books, *Wisdom Jesus,* and the *Wisdom Way of Knowing.* When I searched further, I found and read Marcus Borg's *The Heart of Christianity;* Thomas Keating's *Spirituality, Contemplation, and Transformation;* Pravrajika Vrajaprana's *Vedanta;* Walpola Rahula's *What the Buddha Taught;* Raimon Panikkar's *Christophany;* Helen M. Luke's *Old Age;* Adin Steinsaltz's *The Thirteen Petalled Rose;* and the works of the great Persian Sufi master Jalaluddin Rumi as edited by Kabir Helminski.

Through these teachings, I discovered a deeper understanding of connectedness – unity and oneness bind us. I learned by opening my heart, I could receive help when the going got tough. The essence of Divine love would support me. There was peace. We are never alone. A mystical life force supports us, and through calmness in this knowledge, I was able to move forward. It is time for us to move away from the alienation and polarization of the egocentric operating system and into the unified field of Divine abundance perceived only through the heart. There we will find peace!

While I'm not perfect, I strive to be responsible for my words and actions. I admit when I make a mistake, and work hard at expressing true feelings. Loss quickly puts things into perspective. Loss gives reason to quiet the mind, and then we become thoughtful. In silence, there's rebirth.

My mother's house faces the Columbia River in eastern Washington State. Near the time of her passing, my siblings and I set up a bed in Mom's living room so she could gaze out at the smooth flowing river. On the walls of the room, family photos hung, and we kept calming songs like "Amazing Grace" on the CD player. As my mother neared the time of her death, my brother, sister, nephew, and I placed our hands on her body to give her support. This gesture to her calmed us, too.

The moment of my mother's last breath was an epiphany. Parts of her life flashed before me, and I was, in an instant, reminded of all her special qualities, and the thousands of moments we'd spent together. Could this striking moment have been possible if my heart had not been open to the circle of life and its subtle realms? Making wise choices now insures a quality journey. None of us knows when our short time on the earth is over. *Now* is what matters.

Shortly after my mother died, she returned to communicate her love. She appeared to my friend Dee Jensen. I believe my mother was so evolved she presented herself after death, and conveyed her message to Dee. I asked Dee to describe her experience:

On December 7, 2006, I went to visit my dear friend Lexie in Florida. I was going to be staying in her mother's condominium, and her mother had passed away recently. At the end of the evening of December 8, I awoke quite instantly at approximately five a.m. to see a figure sitting at a desk. I knew this person to be [Lexie's mom] Laura. Laura appeared as a radiant spirit with spectacular rainbow colors all around her. I wasn't afraid, and sensed pure energy flowing in the forms of love, joy, appreciation and gratitude.

I can't say how this was all communicated, nor can I say how Laura spoke to me, but it seemed to be a form of telepathy, or her connection to me without speaking. She wanted me to convey to her son and two daughters that she was very happy; that her life with her children had been loving, beautiful and fulfilling until the very end of her own life. She was now in the afterlife, and excited to be reunited with her husband Mickey. She emphasized her gratitude for the love and friendship of her family, for the meaningful times they'd shared.

The room, with its glow, was stunning – all love. When Laura's spirit faded away and I realized what had just happened, I was moved to tears for several hours. I had never experienced anything like this.

Afterwards, I went to Lexie and told her what happened. Lexie explained how her friends the Buddhist monks had chanted in the condo-

minium. The monks believed a spirit stays on the earth plane for 49 days, sometimes visiting relatives before crossing over. Lexie stated it was a true honor when someone makes herself known this way.

I can tell you that Laura Brockway was a wonderful, spiritually advanced woman. I'm honored her spirit came to me and shared love for Lexie and her siblings. Love transcends all space and time.

When my mom appeared to Dee, who then told me about it, I felt hope and comfort. I learned love never dies. Indeed, love is stronger than death. If I visualize my mom surrounded by a rainbow, I always feel peace. Loss of a loved one does have the power to make us better human beings. Through pain, we're forced to open our hearts, reflect on life's purpose, and tap into other realms.

Another – and higher realm can be found through meditation. In stillness, and by watching our breath, we can move into higher consciousness. On our earth we experience two axes: vertical and horizontal. The vertical axis is the connection we have with the Divine,

and the horizontal our physical being and how we connect with our world. In meditation the mind, free from noise and commotion, makes room to let go of thoughts and worries and moves into a more spacious realm of higher consciousness, and ultimately, peace.

The path to peace includes all traditions. By "traditions" I mean customs, beliefs, values and religions. Personally, I include fellowship in my life that enables me to study, read and connect with other wisdom seekers. Sometimes, when I'm over-extended in my daily schedule and doubt I'll have time to go to class, or read, I take a deep breath and readjust. Classes, research, studying, introspection and reading take time, but the payoff is worth it. It's necessary in the pursuit of a more peaceful planet and self. The quest for knowledge, the exchange of ideas and the sharing of theories are the keys to understanding the nature of peace as it relates to the world and us as a society.

Spiritual knowledge emerges from unlikely arenas, lately even the study of biology. Biology is becoming an information science…and it's only the beginning. When Jonas Salk, developer of the first safe and effective polio vaccine, studied amoebas, he concluded humans would continue to evolve into a less warring nature, toward a kinder communal world. Since Jonas has passed away, unfortunately I can't ask him personally. However, biologists have recently found short-lived patches of amoeba clones contain millions of genetically identical individuals of the species Dictyostelium discoideum. Though they usually live as loners, hunting and eating bacteria, D. discoideum are known to cooperate when food gets scarce and even sacrifice their lives altruistically. Scientists say the discovery of this clonal colony could yield important clues about the evolution of cooperative, peaceful human behavior.

If our leaders could focus on removing conflict, resolving issues, and training their minds to be ever-decisive in these matters, what might happen to disease, hunger and war? This prescription for peace begins with our own serenity and desire. From one to another, peace extends even to world leaders.

In the tradition of world government, I found this five-point peace formula researched and released by UNESCO's Culture of Peace Program, which I hope to see in my – OUR – lifetime:

> *A governmental code of ethics,* with a basis in the Universal Declaration of Human Rights.

> *An international system of justice.* Without justice there can be no peace. Every nation has a system to get criminals off the street, and into the courtroom. A world system of justice is necessary for crimes against humanity and our environment.

> *A global sustainable economy* providing reasonable employment and also eliminating poverty and hunger. According to Nobel Prize-winner Amartya Sen, public peace action can eradicate malnutrition and hunger.

> *Universal access to competent educational systems.* The education of women is key to both economic and peace

developments. Warfare by men has led to the exclusion of women from power. Women's skills of exchange, cooperation and solidarity, as well as their experience giving birth, bringing up the next generation and managing informal economies, are all essential to the evolution of peace cultures.

A compassionate health and welfare system. This principle is included in the Universal Declaration of Human Rights. The more privileged have humanitarian responsibility to help the under-privileged.

Mahatma Gandhi said power is of two kinds: one obtained by fear of punishment, and the other by acts of love. He said power based on love is a thousand times more effective and permanent than power derived from fear of punishment.

Albert Schweitzer, who won the Nobel Peace Prize in 1952, said in one of his most memorable addresses, "Reverence for Life," "I cannot but have reverence for all that is called life. I cannot avoid compassion for everything that is called life. Reverence for life comprises the whole ethic of life in its deepest and highest sense. It is the source of constant renewal for the individual and for all of humankind."

I truly believe visualizing world peace will help bring unity. In visualization, we experience all senses. World-class athletes have been known to visualize mental pictures of upcoming competitions even before they begin. A tennis player may sit in a quiet spot and think about an impending match. He or she would hear the crowd cheering, feel the heat of the courts, envision the ball connecting with the racquet, and feel the weight of the winning trophy as they lift it high over their head in victory.

As a businessperson, I might do a visualization before giving a speech. I will see myself open my heart to the audience, my heart expanding to them, almost embracing the crowd. In everyday life, when my minutes are overloaded – juggling three kids' schedules, sitting down to eat, returning phone calls, spending time with my husband, I retreat. I sit a few minutes on a pillow, close my eyes, watch the breath and visualize peace and complete harmony within my surroundings. Schedules disappear. I find inner peace. I visualize this peaceful reality and it becomes tangible. Such is the power of our perception and creation.

My mother, Laura, told me a story about her work in a mental institution. One of her patients, a German woman, hadn't uttered a word in 20 years. Her so-called muteness had nothing to do with language. She knew English, but simply would not speak. Every day my mother bathed this woman, dressed her, and combed her long hair. After six months alongside my mother, the woman suddenly looked up at her and stammered, "You – are – always – smiling."

When my mother joyously relayed to her co-workers and supervisors what she felt was a breakthrough, they almost laughed. No one believed her. But because of my mother's love, the German woman spoke. My mom's loving smile evoked awareness, and the moment provided a silent woman freedom to speak. This story alone has been a compelling force in my life, and a lesson I have tried to teach my children. Joy and peace are universal truths that must be passed on to the next generation, and the next, and the next. We need to set examples of love, and teach our children that we create peace by the choices we make.

Our thoughts are so powerful in creating reality. When I was 17, I read an insightful book from the nineteenth century called *As a Man Thinketh*, by James Allen. It had such an effect on my own thinking, I carried this tiny yellow book in my purse for years, and re-read it many times. James Allen begins his book: "As a man thinketh, so he is." A person's character is the sum of all his thoughts. Through enlightened thinking, Socratic dialogs, critical inquiry, and an open heart, we can create peace.

Peace has its own energy. What if every thought is a prayer, and every prayer is answered? We can't afford to think negatively. My friend Elliott Curson wrote, "Peace is not having to look over your shoulder." Peace is freedom. Peace is also never looking back. The path behind us is no longer an option. Certainly, we can learn from our mistakes, but now, in this moment, we can conduct our lives with kindness and generosity. Although my copy of *As a Man Thinketh* is weathered and dog eared, the message is still clear: we must steep ourselves in patience and compassion to know the tranquility of the mind.

Why is it headstones at cemeteries list a birth-date, and the date of death? Well, I say the birth-date and date of death are not what matters. It's the dashes in between! We need to live in the dashes with peace.

The spiritual and practical skills to inspire peace emerge from myriad sources. Fourth-century writings of Christ's teachings previously lost from the Bible – unearthed in 1945 near the Egyptian city of Nag Hammadi – are revelatory texts impacting Christianity just as the Dead Sea scrolls shed new light on Judaism. With discoveries of ancient wisdom teachings, we can reeducate ourselves and broaden our perspectives. In receiving the new, we can let go of old patterns. Unconsciousness can become a thing of the past, as we *accept*, and are enlightened.

I was recently made aware of a remarkable woman, researcher Sharry Edwards, pioneering proponent of Human Bio-Acoustics, who has discovered the progression, in sonic frequency, from simple elements to complex life forms. Past efforts were often surrounded with superstition and mysticism, and not until recently computerized and instrumentation developed, allowing her to conclude how certain sounds allow the body to predict and provide for itself, even giving harmony and peace. Her studies and findings are technical, and I don't pretend to understand all of them. What I have learned is that humans have known the importance of certain sounds for a very long time.

Peace even shows up in quantum physics. Robert L. Schrag, PhD, notes: "String theory is a relatively recent development in theoretical physics that reveals the fundamental, irreducible building block of the universe to be an inconceivably tiny vibrating string. Everything is built of these strings. Hence, string theory posits a universe made of music."

Hence, a harmonious universe made of music is a peaceful universe. Music of the spheres! Professor Schrag's work examines the implications of string theory in a landscape seen as remote from physics – the human heart. As such it is an exploration of string theory in the harmonic nature of life, existence, love, God and the universe.

To keep tranquility and harmony present in my marriage, my husband and I take walks into town, or within the forest. We cultivate and appreciate our gardens. When I'm on horseback I see lupine, bluebirds, and rushing rivers. I find nature to be a great *consulter*. We create our own peace. We surround ourselves with good friends, kind and impeccable in their words. I don't feel good listening to gossip, or dishonesty. Our windows let in beautiful sunlight. The colors in our home are soft and soothing: yellows, pinks, greens, soft reds. Our cats purr in our laps, the dogs run outside, and we often have friends over for dinner, for fellowship and exchange of ideas. In my house, I've created a small space where I can sit on a small pillow and quiet my mind, find personal peace when I need it.

How will you begin? Perhaps you have a study, or a special chair in a tranquil part of your home. What creates peace for you? Food plays an important role in my health, and for the most part we eat organic. At night my children, husband and I take time to tell stories, and to reflect upon our day.

Like a superb Anatoly Ivanov mosaic, we are called to create a new masterpiece within ourselves, and within our world. We all hold a piece in creating peace. One person's peace will extend to another, and another, and another. My mother would say, "Peace is like the perfume you wear. It lingers and affects everyone you meet."

My hope is this: After you read these thoughtful responses to peace, you will move to a deeper level within your own heart. Truth and peace are not defended; they are lived. May peace be our intention and purpose in this lifetime.

Lexie Potamkin

Before you read on, take a moment to look into your own heart and soul, and answer the question...

WHAT IS PEACE?

"Peace is when our life priorities are in balance with our behavior. Our love of God, love of family, love of endeavor and very important, the love of self."

A.J. Scribante, Entrepreneur, executive

"Peace is forgiveness and non-judgment. I believe everyone deserves a second chance."

Adam Potamkin

"Holding hands with fingers entwined. Sleeping warmly in the arms of someone you love."

Aizik Wolf, Neurosurgeon

"The question itself suggests that peace is a singular thing, and that it can be defined. Peace is a confluence of many things that are different for many people. But ultimately we will all arrive at a certain 'feeling' or 'moment' in our lives and we recognize it as peace and will hopefully grab it and preserve it in our hearts and minds. At this point the feeling is absorbed to be slowly squeezed back out.

"I belong to a group of incredibly dedicated people known as the Castaways against Cancer. Each year since 2000, they have kayaked from Key Biscayne, Florida to Key West, Florida to raise money for the American Cancer Society. I went on the trip last year and just returned from the trek this year. That's 170 miles in 7 days. Twenty five miles a day averaging about ten hours a day. That's 155,000 strokes of a paddle to get there. Every one of them painful. On day five you're blistered, beaten, sore and ready to give out. Alone on the water surrounded by nature that has been there a thousand years before you, absolute quiet is the rule. As the boat glides through the water, forty feet away a giant sea turtle floats. As you pass he just looks gently at the boat and you. He submerges ever so slowly and then he's gone.

"The feeling that went through me at that point was pure peace. The fact that nothing in this world makes sense made all my thoughts click together like the last digit in a combination lock. Peace was there and I grabbed it.

"I don't suggest everybody take the trip but I can tell you that peace is out there, and you'll know it when it's in front of you. And when the time comes, grab it and it will be in you and yours to share forever."

Adam Scholer, English teacher for 20 years

"Harmony and balance without aggression."

Alan Sirkin, Real estate investments

"Life is filled with moments of joy, moments of challenge, and moments of sorrow. Peace is found within the framework of each individual's capacity to isolate their destiny Once achieved, their use of that position is to reach out and help others."

Amber Marie Brookman

"Peace begins with each one of us. Peace is having good feelings inside.'

Alice Gabsi

"When the mind is filled with the absence of thought. When the mind experiences utter calm. When the mind is aware that the essence of love is all that it experiences. When the mind is aware that nothing exists beyond love. When two opposite forces join in love and compassion."

Alicia Sirkin, Founder, The Sirkin Creative Living Center

"Inner peace is loving yourself. It's the dancing and stillness in one's own shadows and light. It's knowing who you are. It's the welcoming and receiving of inner connectedness. It's relating one's essence to others; to our planet, to consciousness, to vision, to spirit.

"Family peace is being open to the fullest and deepest measure of loving and being loved. It's seeing the ones you love, both reflected in yourself, and as completely distinct and unique, and using that mirror and that differential for the highest growth and potential.

"Global peace is communities working together to both respect difference and make a stand for history. It's recognizing our humanity and our connection to each other. It's seeing the tapestry of the human race unfold, appreciating its components, and seeing both the whole, and the weave between.

"Global peace is within our reach. We only need to recognize that peace is possible. And that the responsibility and mandate is ours."

Dr. Amy Friedman, Psychologist

"Peace is feeling so much love: blankness in my heart. Deep feelings, where I have just let go of everything, once and for all. I am just Amy. Not any more, not any less."

Amy Tessier, Artist working in oil and paper-mache

⊛

"Politically: brief periods of time characterized by an absence of war. History doesn't know long lasting peace between countries. Emperor Augustus is praised by historians for keeping Romans from waging war against neighbors for thirty years—the longest in European history. Peace in political times isn't attainable.

"Peace is a sweet dream of humanity.

"Peace which dwells within ourselves, best known as being at peace with yourself.

"It's often mentioned by people, but very seldom experienced— and only with certain training and meditation. People aren't designed and created to be in peace.

"Life in peace is a pure harmony which doesn't exist.

"The best manifestation of peace would be a sleeping baby— totally innocent and completely at peace with itself.

"That is why we smile looking at this child and feel a moment of peace."

Anatoly Ivanov, Artist and friend

"When I was 10 years old, Lexie asked me the question of questions: What is spirit? It was all so simple then. I wrote a poem explaining what, in my mind, was the world's greatest definition of spirit, and it even rhymed!

"Now, almost a decade later, Lexie has another question: What is peace? I wish I could call my ten-year-old self and ask her. I tried to write something clever, cute or funny but I am scared and I am stuck. Then, I realized, peace is what I felt defining spirit. Peace is feeling comfortable with yourself and your thoughts, without fear of judgment or rejection.

"Peace is being able to answer one of life's greatest questions in a rhyme."

Andi Potamkin, Dreamer

"Peace is balance—order out of chaos.

"It's the most important essence to living a healthy life. It doesn't matter where you're from, what your religion is, or your status. Having inner peace finds everything that's ahead is clear. Clarity will guide us to be fair to everybody and everything; to respect the world around us.

"It's part of my daily prayer for my daughter, neighbor, family, friends, and society. It's the basic ingredient to being happy."

Anna M. Torres, Flight attendant–international

"Peace is when you feel relaxed."

Anika Ramchandani

"For me, the concept of peace means a sense of equilibrium and empowerment in my relationship with the world that results in a feeling of calm and contentment. My sense of peace is very much related to my reaction to and attitude about what is happening in the present, and my ability to learn from and let go of the past.

"The goal of achieving a constant feeling of peace is a work in progress for me; but the journey toward this destination facilitates and enhances my ability to feel calm in the midst of chaos, optimistic in the midst of strife, content in the midst of challenges, and pro ductive in the midst of distractions.

"Goodwill and respect for self and others are inherent in the quest for inner peace. If each of us individually strives for peace, then together we could ultimately achieve that elusive ideal state of relationships in the world--global peace."

Anita Zatz, Speech pathologist

"There is no road towards peace; peace is the road."

Mahatma Gandhi

9

"Peace is beauty. Peace is love.

"Peace is a meadow filled with goldenrod with the sun shinning brightly. It's a sky filled with stars and a full moon with a beaming face.

"Peace is a world without conflict, with individuals united without fear—believing love is more important than hate, jealously, or destruction."

Arleen Race Wolf, Artist-sculptor

"Instead of defining peace, I'm writing about how to achieve world peace.

"We don't have world peace because we lack respect and understanding for the rest of the people in this world.

"If we can send every young man or woman, for one year, to another country then we can increase respect and understanding for each other exponentially. These young people can go to any foreign country of their choice. Young people from the United States can go to China, Russia, Africa, Middle East, or even Canada or Mexico. They can go for a year of college, backpacking, or social work. It doesn't matter. They'll come back with an understanding that we're more alike than different. Imagine the impact of hundreds of thousands of young people roaming the world and building bridges of understanding."

Atul S. Thakkar, President and CEO Attronica

"The obvious answer is no war and all good people getting along in harmony. Peace comes to me watching a child, or any person, laughing uncontrollably. A puppy playing. A sunrise over the ocean. Husband and dog sleeping contently the moment before they both wake."

Barbara Zweig, Retired wall street executive

"Peace of Mind: The mind is at peace when you know the children you have brought into this world are safe, sound and living up to their fullest potential.

"Peace of Heart: The heart is full and at peace when you come to rest each night with the one you love, or the comforting memories they left behind.

"Peace of Soul: The soul finds peace in the belief that there is a future that is free of mindless hate—where the world is a community that thrives on tolerance and diversity."

Barry Nelson, Estate planning attorney
Judith Nelson, Mediator

"Peace is a state that is rarely achieved. It occurs in the absence of contention—when people agree on a course of action or a given lifestyle. Peace can be achieved among a family, a neighborhood, a school, a city, a nation, or the world. Whatever the unit of measure, the key factor is the lack of discord, the basic agreement among the people therein."

Edward G. Rendell, Governor of Pennsylvania

"Peace is being happy that your friends and family are fine:- healthy, happy, striving, to improve their education, job or if they're sick responding to their medicine.

"Peace is also seeing the progress of the children that I'm treating.

"Peace brings harmony—a desire to engage and assist others."

Bea Alberelli, Occupational therapist

"As a Christian, I believe true peace comes from God. The scriptures tell us that God's peace goes beyond all understanding. This is why, even when I'm going through troublesome times, there is a heavenly calmness in my soul that keeps me even through situations I cannot change.

"Peace is described in one of my favorite hymns: 'When peace like a river attendeth my soul; when sorrows like sea billows roll; whatever my lot, Thou has taught me to say – it is well, it is well with my soul.'

"How does one get this peace? Simply by asking our Heavenly Father. You will know He has answered you when you feel the warmth of His love. In times of trouble peace is the calmness of the Lord's voice saying, 'Let not your heart be troubled'."

Bea L. Hines, Retired journalist, *The Miami Herald*

"Peace is a qualitative agreement converting conflicting aspirations into related efficiencies. Once subscribed to the notion that the aim of life is productivity for one's mind, family, culture, and organization, it becomes clear that peace represents the foundation that allows our purpose to progress. Identifying, understanding, and cradling commonalities allows myself, and the community around me, to better expedite our necessities and intended achievements because the opportunity for cooperation and coordination is unobstructed.

"These compromising gestures provide a destination we all hope to reach."

Benjamin McFerren, Media activist

✿

"Peace is a word of kindness. Whenever you use peace, peace is what you shall get in return. Those who fought with each other in the past and who are now best friends receive the touch of peace. The person who gave them that touch of peace is God, Himself. Although God gave the peace, it is our job to spread it. That is what peace means to me."

Bradley Hull, age 9, honored by his school for this paragraph on peace

✿

15

"Peace is a state of mind, a way of being that is born out of confidence and contentment. Peaceful living involves trusting that other people's race, gender, religion and ethnicity is as important to them as yours is to you. Out of this kind of trust comes the natural tendency to accept. Acceptance goes beyond tolerance. Acceptance is comfort, and comfort is peaceful. When projected onto the global community, this confident, content, trusting and comfortable way translates into a safer world."

Diane Goodman, Caterer, Fisher Island Day School chef, fiction writer

"Peace is a feeling you experience when you are making a substantial difference in the communities you serve and where you live. I feel peace when I help make a difference.

"One of my biggest dreams is that everyone in this world sees how important it is to put their little grain of sand to do wonderful actions by fomenting and practicing world peace."

Daniella Ortiz Baeza, Fashion designer and director
of Development, Nova Southeastern Universal

"What is peace?

"Peace is the state of being which exists within an open flow of communication between one's conscious thought and his personal source of divine inspiration, be it God, Buddha or 'The Light.'

"Peace is also found in the knowing that angels are at work in this world, urging us to articulate our own interpretations of 'spirit' and 'peace' so that we might join together, in an inspired form of group prayer."

Claudia Potamkin, Broadcast announcer, musician, racecar driver, community activist

"Peace is calm inward quietness. Peace is the space in your mind above the constant chatter that enters your mind from our chaotic world. Peace is egoless. It emanates from the stillness of your soul."

Clifford T. Salomon, Neurosurgeon, co-founder, Angels of the Or

"Peace is when my soul is able to tap the spirit of the universe. The flow of harmony, serenity and compassion allows me to feel 'heaven is on earth.'"

Craig Drake, Jewelry manufacturer

"I'm struck by the realization that the simplicity of the question belies the complexity of the subject. Seeking a way to narrow the scope to frame a response I am drawn to the Greek Philosopher Epictetus (c. AD 55-135), who found it useful to argue that inner peace was attainable only by philosophy and not by worldly pursuits: 'You must be busy either with your inner man, or with things outside, that is, you must choose between the position of a philosopher and that of an ordinary man.'

"Returning to Epictetus, could it be that in today's contest he was wrong and that the path to peace in the 21st Century must be illuminated not only by worldly pursuits but by this new theologically inspired philosophy? And if that is true, could it be that the achievement of inner peace is not distinct from the attainment of world peace but is now a pre-requisite for it?

"If those arguments have any merit, peace can then be defined as the absence of conflict among peoples, made possible through their individual pursuit of inner peace."

Diego E. Hernandez, Vice Admiral, U.S. Navy (Retired)

"Send Thy peace, O Lord, which is perfect and everlasting, that our souls may radiate peace. Send Thy peace, O Lord, that we may think, act, and speak harmoniously. Send Thy peace, O Lord, that we may be contented and thankful for Thy bountiful gifts. Send Thy peace, O Lord, that amidst our worldly strife we may enjoy thy bliss. Send Thy peace, O Lord, that we may endure all, tolerate all in the thought of thy grace and mercy. Send Thy peace, O Lord, that our lives may become a divine vision, and in Thy light all darkness may vanish. Send Thy peace, O Lord, our Father and Mother, that we Thy children on earth may all unite in one family. Amen."

Hazrat Inayat Khan, Sufi spiritual guide

"I say we achieve strength through peace. That's the new doctrine I'm going to promote."

Dennis Kucinich, Congressman proposing a Department of Peace

"Peace is no wars.
Peace is kind actions.
Peace is a big heart.
Peace is beautiful.
Peace is Iraq and the United States making amends.
Peace is the sun setting on a beautiful Saturday night at the beach.
Peace is towering trees, looking down on us like the Empire
    State Building.
Peace is a family, loving and caring for each other.
Peace is a couple, together at a romantic dinner, sharing happiness.
Peace is everything positive.
Nothing negative is peaceful.
Peace is beautiful."

Cole Potamkin

"Knowing all my children are safe
Having more friends than enemies
Realizing how beautiful my sunsets are and watching the moon
Having all my dogs asleep and loving me "

Dollie Cole, Texas rancher

"During WWII, many of the young men of my neighborhood were in the armed forces and our small section of Brooklyn was particularly unlucky in terms of casualties. During the last year of the war, seven of our friends from the neighborhood were killed, and many others were seriously hurt. Still others were in the Philippines preparing to invade Japan, where heavy losses were expected. The world seemed gray. I remember the day in early August of 1945 when the news arrived that Japan had surrendered. The war was over. At that moment, peace to me was a simple matter; my friends were safe; no one else was going to die. It was peace."

Donald Forman, Retired educator

"Peace is the acceptance of the imperfection of the Self."

Dorothy Thau, Parapsychologist, reader,
holistic health counselor

"The absence of war might be one indicator that peace prevails. But life doesn't stop long enough for us to fasten on a moment of peace and declare we have peace. The process of living entails ongoing challenges, with which we must contend – sometimes to respond to threats of force here at home or from abroad, or to assure that our families can be provided for, or to adapt to changes in the planet on which we live.

"The measure of peace is determined by the quality of our response to these continuing challenges. When our response deepens injustice, peace is at risk. When we ignore environmental changes that can be harmful, peace is at risk. When as a nation we violate international rules, peace is at risk.

"Thus I define peace as the adherence to the rule of law and to those institutions that serve justice and the support of those instruments of government that act wisely in pursuit of the common good. When our institutions strive to advance the public welfare and do away with injustice, and when we refrain from the use of force except where no other course is left, then we may consider we have peace. But only so long as these conditions prevail."

Donald M. Fraser, Attorney,
State Senator 1955-1961
U.S. House of Representatives 1963-1978
Mayor of Minneapolis 1980-1993

"When your soul and body are in complete communion with the love of God, there you have complete peace."

Edesa Valdes, Retired airline employee.

"Peace first comes from deep inside the spirit. Then it's projected outwards towards society—creating tranquility throughout the rest of the world."

Dr. Dave Jensen, Sports chiropractor, founder of W.I.N. Institute

"Peace is not having to look over your shoulder."

Elliott Curson, Advertising executive

"In a world without harmony there is no peace. In a world without love there is no peace. In a world without balance there is no peace. In a world without sharing there is no peace. Peace is the abundance of all of the above."

Gustavo Novoa, Artist, painter

"Look at the face of newborn babies and see the essence of peace dwelling in their eyes.

"Peace is the touch of an innocent child learning to take his first steps. Peace lies within the heart and soul of every individual—not in the outward reaches of the limited mind.

"Peace is the beauty and grace of a contented soul flying on the wings of a Godly song. Peace is the sustenance, the music, the sunrise and sunset of a life of joy. It's bliss lived with benevolence and generosity of spirit. Peace is the quiet, calm, stillness of happiness revealed with love for our fellowman."

Etta Stevens, Meditation teacher, writer, former radio talk show host, jewelry designer

"From a Buddhist perspective, sustainable peace between peoples of the world must emerge from peace-of-mind within each and every person in the world. This can't be imposed or enforced. It must come from within. Buddhist meditation helps us quell inner destructive emotions, thoughts, and habits. Meditation helps us calm the harsh winds of anger, greed, jealousy and ignorance that stir up the surface of our ocean-like minds. It helps our minds to rest in the deep calm currents of compassionate consciousness that underlie the passionate tempests that cause mental unrest. Once we're in a state of inner peace, the violence of the world can't shake us, and we become an example for others to follow.

"From an InterSpiritual perspective, inner peace can be generated by the profound contemplative practices found within each of the world's religions. It is through these practices that we can experience a shared spiritual experience with all peoples everywhere. Once we rest in this state together, we will never see each other as 'the other,' for we are bonded within the shared essence of our being. This is the foundation for peace throughout the world. Generating this form of inner and outer peace is the goal of our Spiritual Paths Foundation and our program on InterSpiritual Wisdom."

Dr. Ed Bastian, President, Spiritual Paths Foundation

"Behold but One in all things; it is the second that leads you astray."

Kabir

"Peace is a state of mind you enjoy when your life is respectful of the standards of morality, ethics and humanity. That means it isn't necessary to spend energy to see what's behind you. You can then focus on what's ahead."

Eugene L. Gitin, Retired physician

"Since the beginning of time, peace may be mankind's most illusive search. Wars are fought in the name of peace. Lands are conquered so people can live in peace. Armies are formed to keep peace. In this vast search to find peace, the nearness of it isn't seen.

"Inner peace, as beauty, is in the mind and command of the individual. Peace is in a child's eye as they experience their first smile; in the vibrant color of leaves on trees in the Fall season; in a church service praying for peace—enjoying a night of star gazing.

"Peace is in and all around mankind, and, as we voyage through life, it is we who must pass this peace on in the name of peace."

Frank A Salvatore, Former Pennsylvania State Senator

"Peace is the most important feeling to achieve. We achieve peace when we feel and give love instead of anger.

"If you have inner peace you can do anything."

Gene Adcock, Marble and bronze sculptor

"Peace is the comfort you find from your loving family at the end of each day."

George Spalina, Chief Financial Officer
Potamkin Auto Group Manhattan

"When there is gentleness in the world; when you see yourself in someone else. That is peace. Each endeavoring. All achieving."

Gerald Cope, Architect

"Peace is indeed one of the five intrinsic qualities of the spirit. It's our original nature. Peace is the garland around our necks, so to speak. All one needs to do is to step inside.

"There's a story about a queen who kept looking for her heart necklace when all along, it was around her neck. Peace at times is like that. We keep looking everywhere for it. However, it's inside.

"Let's gently step inside, remove the debris, remind the self. I am a being of peace. Peace is my birthright. I am peace."

Gita Stevenson, Social worker, also does dance therapy

"The true nature of peace lies in the emptiness between thoughts."

Fernando Valverde, Assistant Dean College of Medicine,
Florida International University

"There are two kinds of peace; inner and outer. Inner peace is contentment and self acceptance of the oneness of all. Outer peace is living with an open heart."

Myrna Rae Bartell Pettit

"This question brings to mind two quotes. First, the Dalai Lama. 'Although attempting to bring about world peace through the internal transformation of individuals is difficult, it is the only way.'

"The second quote comes from theologian Dietrich Bonhoeffer. 'Peace must be dared. It's the great venture. It can never be safe. Peace is the opposite of security. To demand guarantees is to mistrust. To look for guarantees is to want to protect oneself. Peace means to give oneself altogether to the law of God, wanting no security—not trying to direct it for selfish purposes.'

"For me peace is more about harmony, congruence, authenticity and integrity, and not about the absence of conflict or a feeling of calm. When I'm living in harmony with the universal urge toward life and love, when I'm living with integrity, in congruence with my deepest values, then I'm living from my most authentic self, and I'm at peace. When I'm at peace, I'm available to the universe to be used for peaceful ends.

"Currently, I'm technically homeless. Having recently lost my full-time job, I'm unable to afford an apartment and I'm relying on others for shelter. My temporary stay is due to end in a month, and I have no idea where I will be going next.

"This morning it occurred to me to change my prayer from 'I need another place to stay' to 'God, where do you want us to live next?' That change reminded me into whose hands I've commended my spirit and put me back in touch with the peace that is always there."

Gigi Ross

"Peace is a feeling of calm and satisfaction. No worries, no anxiety, no guilt.
Satisfaction is peace.
Peace is knowing you chose right from wrong.
Peace is forgiving and forgetting.
Peace is loving and cherishing.
Peace is having faith and trust.
Being in balance is peace."

Grace Wong, Finance

"Peace is the rekindling of the human spirit. It's the place within each of ourselves that is most like children. It's revealed through love of oneself. Peace is the ultimate Divine of the universe."

Greg Rettman, Filmmaker, activist, writer, author, producer, director

"Peace is a feeling or state of mind which enables one to feel calm, at ease and secure. Peace is forever elusive—it comes and goes—never dwelling everywhere at the same time. Peace is in the minds of humans from time to time."

Herbert M. Frank, Retired business owner

"I went to many Indian bazaars.
I went to huge American shopping malls.
I dived deep down into the Atlantic Ocean.
In fact, I was in search for peace.

I sat on the peak of snowy Mountains.
I stayed in the thick sandalwood forest.
I took flights for higher up in the sky.
In fact, I was in search for peace.

I bought many new clothes.
I tried lots of different dishes.
I drink Coke, Pepsi and lemonade.
In fact, I was in search for peace.

I traveled to many holy sites.
I lit many bright lamps.
I tried to save ants under my feet.
In fact, I was in search for peace.

I went to Stupa with prostration and scarf.
I went into temple with flowers and coconut .
I went to churches with faith and rosary.
In fact, I was in search for peace.

Unfortunately, there is no mall for peace.
There is no tree that ripens peace.
No place to pick up peace that I yearn for.
No matter how hard I tried.

I referred back to Buddha's teaching,
He said, 'No sages can wash your negativities.
They don't dispel sufferings with their hands,
But, liberate by revealing the true nature of things.'

Finding no other way I sit down on my cushion.
I listen to the teachings and contemplate.
I meditate and practice on the long path for peace.
There it is. I find just a reflection of peace.

Peace is a radiance within ourselves.
Peace that benefits one and all."

Geshe Tsuglag Gyatso

"You are peace, as the natural state is peaceful.

"Man's nature is divine, and peace, therefore, is within. A calm and peaceful mind sees peace everywhere, as it reflects the Divine in you on the mirror of your mind.

"Because our natural state is peaceful, one only has to avoid disturbing it. As a result it is important to control your mind, by keeping your thoughts peaceful and staying away from those who would disturb that peace.

"Since the most powerful energy on earth is thought force, it becomes clear, that one should stay away from disturbing thoughts. In a very real way we are what we think we are. The path to peace is through the knowledge of the Divine. Moreover, when your mind is peaceful and your life and emotions are in balance, everything flows harmoniously through grace. By maintaining a calm and peaceful mind you can experience your pure self, which is the self and hence self-realization. By experiencing that self, the labels we wear fall away, and life becomes a joy, for peaceful people are secure and don't hurt others, or cause pain and suffering.

"Finally, being peaceful means to live the pretend, as the past forfeits the vitality of your life, and the future may never be. Keep your peace at all costs, and you will live a dedicated life. You are peace as the real you is peaceful. Man's nature is divine; therefore peace and the kingdom of God are within. If you master your mind you will see friends everywhere rather than enemies.

"There is but one spirit and it is within that spirit that we can come together in peace."

Dr. Gail Gross, Teacher, psychologist, author

"Peace is watching the sunrise while listening
to the ocean's voice.
It's sitting still, allowing the world to enter your being.
Feeling the sun warm your skin.
Hearing the birds sing their early morning song.
Seeing a new day unfold as the mist burns away.
Smelling the freshness of flowers blooming.
Peace is looking at a sleeping child, and
the calmness his face reflects,
It's the stillness in your home when you first
awake early in the morning.
The feeling of harmony in the deepest chamber
of your being, your soul.
Peace is a choice; peace is life, and peace is love."

Jessica Bruno, Teacher, martial artist, gardener

"Peace is not being consumed by what other people think.

Peace is comfort and often joy of being with those who are different from ourselves.

Peace is not looking past one's shoulder to see who is coming in the room.

Peace is choosing yourself as the first person you would like to be with.

Peace is silence without anxiousness.

Peace is reacting with love.

Peace is letting it be the way it is.

Peace is the rhythm of one foot in front of the other.

Peace feeling vulnerable and showing it.

Peace is paying attention to your children, spouse and friends without trying to control them.

Peace is relishing small pleasures.

Peace is reaching the summit and not having to show the photos.

Peace is community at work.

Peace is napping through a thunderstorm.

Peace is vigilance with your integrity and forgiving yourself when it slips.

Peace is not being too big or too small, but the right size.

Peace is one place, though the path and destination look different to each of us."

Gretchen Cole, Mother, formerly in travel and conservation

"My life has mantras as anchors. I didn't hesitate for a second when I heard the word 'peace'. Albeit there are many forms of peace, one that applies in a world of so many occasions and interactions is: 'Forgive yourself. Forgive the other persons And then move forward'.

"Forgive yourself first because in many cases we may feel we're the victim. In reality we're a big part, if not the largest part of the equation since we generally put ourselves in these situations by free will.

"If that's the case forgive the other person, their faults or lack of being what you expected. Then last but not least, let go.

"It's the past and it's unchangeable. Go forward with forgiveness and preparedness."

Ivan Skoric, Real estate sales, painter

"Peace to me is being serene in one's own body.
Peace to me is inner self peace with one's looks, achievements and goals.
Peace to me is not being envious of others.
Peace to me is enjoyment.
Peace to me is having a good attitude.
But overall, peace to me is my family; children and the unconditional love from each."

Jack Langer, Natural gas consultant

"I am the mother of a 2-year old beautiful girl and 6-year old handsome boy, wife to an amazing husband, and keeper of a lovely home. Before that I was a certified massage therapist and a certified colon hydrotherapist. Going to work was much easier than the super full-time mom job—but the super full-time mom job is the best job I could ever have been given.

"Peace to me is many things and at this moment I feel that it is making time for me to be alone or doing a yoga class, taking a relaxing bath, taking a walk and listening to the sounds of nature—something that is just for me. Next is quality time for my husband, family, friends and community, and all in the right balance of time.

"Peace is holding my sleeping children, laughing with them every day, looking in their eyes and seeing them for the special spirits that they are. When I look into their eyes I feel awe and light, and I'm in the perfect moment.

"Peace is taking a time out from the news, commercials, not consuming things I don't really need, and not allowing myself to feel the pressure to buy more of the stuff I really don't need."

Jacqueline Parker Skoric

"Peace is harmony. It's a state of being. The Yoga Patanjali says that it can only be achieved when the body, mind, and spirit (often likened to three wild horses, each pulling in a different direction) are linked as one. It's only when they are brought under control can we be in peace.

"Each of us has within us both the cause of unrest and the solution. Peace can only be achieved by working on ourselves. It is not to be found in solving other people's or nation's problems if we haven't first solved our own. If we're at peace within ourselves the world will be at peace."

Jane Werner Aye, Writer and appraiser of Asian art

"The sound of your precious children sleeping quietly.
The sound of the ocean waves crashing along the beach.
The sound of family and friends around the dinner table
    exchanging stories, laughter and tears.
The sound of the wind rushing through pine trees and coconut
    palms.
The sound of snow swishing under your skis.
Knowing all your loved ones are home safe and sound.
Silence and noise in equal measures."

Janet Black Larson, Australian, Aspen ski concierge
for Australian tour company, mother

"Peace is heaven here on earth – total tranquility. For different moments such as watching a sunrise on a secluded beach, or seeing a moon rise when it is full over a vast and calm sea from the side of an ocean liner vessel.

"For me, the one moment that is as close to total tranquility and the feeling of 'peace' is on the flight deck of an aircraft ascending 'towards the heaven' like a 'homesick angel' in a dense fog/cloud layer early in the morning and piercing through 'the top' and entering the blue-reddish-orange clear sky of the early hours with the fluffy billowy blanket of white undercast below getting farther and farther away beneath."

Javier Ferrea, CEO of Zero Eight Papa, Crew Your Jet Aviation Corp.

"Peace is what we all seek in life, but only a few are fortunate enough to find and experience it. I believe that to recognize the true meaning and sensation of peace one must overcome many obstacles in life to elevate you to a higher level filled with knowledge and light. Once found it should just become part of your lifestyle where all of your thoughts, emotions and actions are in harmony. It is achieved when your inner force of energy is connected with your exterior and there is a complete sense of satisfaction happiness, acceptance, tranquility and even strength.

"It is what prepares us to depart peacefully from this world."

Jean L. Labrada-Sbert, Business owner

"I researched the definition of peace and found this Chinese proverb: 'If there is righteousness in the heart there will be beauty in the character. If there be beauty in the character, there will be harmony in the home. If there is harmony in the home, there will be order in the nation. When there is order in the nation, there will be peace in the world.'

"When we think of peace we must think of peace of mind, harmony at home, order, righteousness, character and a stable environment. Today's world is hectic. The news is biased towards sensationalism. The world economy is in trouble. Oil prices are escalating. We are in a recession—not a great time for peace.

"Religion, peace, harmony, righteousness and order. We have been taught these values in all religions, and yet religious beliefs have started almost all the wars for 2000 years. What is actually being taught in the world? Certainly not 'Love thy neighbor.' The only way to really have peace in the world is through education. Unfortunately, it will take years to teach people understanding and harmony.

"Is peace in the world possible? Maybe."

Jeffrey Orleans, Chairman and CEO, Orleans Homebuilders

"Peace is the inner feeling you get when you're happy with yourself in knowing that you have given happiness to others, especially family and friends."

Jerry Blavat, Entertainer

"Peace is global sustainability. Global sustainability—meeting today's economic and environmental needs, while preserving the options for future generations to meet theirs—is the greatest challenge to peace in the 21st century and beyond. If we continue with 'business as usual,' the earth's average temperature will probably rise between 3.6° to 8.1°F by 2100. The consequence will be broad-based disruption of the global ecology and economy, including: increased storm devastation; intense heat waves and droughts; and inundated coastal cities. The worst case: a melting of half of the Antarctic and Greenland ice sheets causing a worldwide sea level rise of up to 20 feet. The result will be massive human migrations, global economic chaos, and intense civil unrest and war.

"This scenario will be further exacerbated by the 'perfect storm' that drove oil prices up to well over $100 a barrel and gas over $4 a gallon at the pump. This furious energy storm is fueled by an oil demand that will soon exceed the supply; by increasing consumption in China and India; and by the 'geopolitics of scarcity' which has put oil under siege in hot spots like Iran, Iraq, Nigeria, Saudi Arabia and Venezuela.

"The only permanent solution to the energy-climate crisis is a bold international initiative to accelerate the imperative transition from the fossil fuel era to the age of an abundant renewable hydrogen economy. Global sustainability is essential to building an enduring world peace."

Jerry B. Brown, Ph.D., Anthropologist, educator, energy expert, public speaker, co-author of *Freedom from Mid-East Oil*

"Peace is when you find a balance with yourself. It's the place you can return to despite apparent chaos. Peace is the ability to create the harmony and equilibrium while floating in a world of perpetual change/instability."

Jennifer Tchinnosian, Student, journalist, freethinker

"Peace is being able to enjoy all that surrounds us without fearing anything. It's the tranquility that comes with the unfettered enjoyment of family, friends and all of the world's beauty. There's a quiet calm that comes with peace."

Jerome S. Tilis, Retired media executive

"To me, peace is watching my children sleeping comfortably in their warm, dry beds, knowing that I have the means to love, care for and provide for them. I am so thankful that I live in a place where I have the freedom and the means to protect them. This intense, deep-rooted love we have for our babies is something that parents all around the world have in common. But not everyone has the ability to shield their kids from cold hunger and harm. I am so grateful and that brings me peace."

Jo Ann Tollefson, Mother and substitute teacher

"For us peace is Inner peace. It is a state of mind, a state of higher consciousness where there are no words or thoughts, no guilt or grievances—no conflicts, no separation or judgments, no interpretations that occupies a timeless moment.

"This peace is a gift from God, our Creator, and is always within us. It has nothing to do with external events or the state of our bodies. It is a consciousness where you feel safe, loving, fully loved and restful. It is where there are no exclusions of your love and that you experience a Oneness that has no beginning or ending. This state of Inner peace is so interlaced with love and joy that they can not be separated from each other because they are one and the same. It is a state of mind that experiences the presence of heaven.

"Peace is state of consciousness that is beyond any words that could possibly describe it, and is one with its source. It is a state of mind where there is only light and no darkness, pain or suffering. It is a state of defenselessness where there is no desire to hurt others or yourself. It is state where nothing is of value except the peace, joy and love that you are. It is a consciousness where spirit and soul are fused into one and where the essence of peace, love and joy are known beyond belief as our only true identity."

Jerry Jampolsky, M.D. and Diane Cirincione, Ph.D.,
Authors of a mini course for Life and Finding Our Way Home

૭

"Peace is the miracle of a sleeping newborn baby.
Peace is having faith that God loves you.
Peace is the gift of hope you receive when you see your
    children's children receive their own peace.
Peace is received from the charity of helping people.
Peace is receiving grace as you are ready to see God."

Jim and Ginny Hibler, Retired from a lifetime in the food service
equipment industry and raising a family

"Peace is doing the right thing, regardless of the consequences.

"We humans are three people: The person whom others think we are, the person whom we think we are, the person whom we really are. Peace is living congruent with the latter. Peace is living without pretense."

Jim D. Pruitt, Commodity futures trader

"Harmony with oneself. Free of anger, anxiousness, envy and despair."

John Bruno, Automobile executive

"Peace is nourishment for the soul. It's that part of us that we are born with, and knowing that space and place of total stillness. The silence of being in nature and connecting to that higher power. Using the ability to transform negative into positive. Being able to experience being free from all obstacles. Finding contentment anywhere and everywhere under all circumstances.

"The more you experience peace through consciousness and awareness, the more it becomes a part of you. Then your gift is to share this with others. It shines through you and your energy of peace opens up the hearts of all."

Joanne W. Haahr, Connects and
collaborates with people.

✿

"Peace is a state of equilibrium where two or more parties can coexist and pursue their own objectives with respect, dignity, and compassion. Peace is also a state of mind where harmony exists amidst tension.

"Peace is a goal to which we all strive and rarely achieve, but the pursuit of this goal is nonetheless paramount to both internal and external forces that are always potentially in conflict."

John Glick, Medical oncology

✿

"Peace is hope and love fulfilled."

Joe Fetzer, General Motors executive (retired)

"When we say we want peace on earth, we're really talking about reducing conflict in people's minds. War is an ancient activity, and so is the dilemma of dealing with our minds. To cultivate peace, we must first become familiar with it. In peaceful abiding meditation, we follow the breath in order to enter the present moment and rest there. Emotions and thoughts are still coming up, but with less power to drag us into anger and jealousy. We glimpse the tranquility, clarity, and steadiness underneath our mental drama. That's peace: a clean and clear mind that we can take into every activity. Although relatively few people in the world are meditating, if we have the inspiration and courage to say, 'It's up to me to bring peace;' our influence will soon be larger than our numbers."

Sakyong Mipham Rinpoche, Leader of Shambhala, author

"Many people define peace as the opposite of war. Still others would define peace as a phenomenon impossible to witness in our diverse and modern world.

"I have a personal definition of peace. My peace comes from spending my days creating the opportunity for education, and with it the potential for freedom for children.

"As the founder of Room to Real, an organization dedicated to bringing literacy to the world's children, my vision of peace is a world in which children are given a chance to learn. To me, the knowledge that children gain when they learn about themselves and the world around them is the surest path to a world where we appreciate each other's differences and recognize our universal oneness. Peace."

John Wood, Founder and CEO, Room to Read

"Peace is no hatred. A world where everyone can be friends. Sadly, only astronauts – who see one world from far in space – can see and understand that we are really one people living on one planet. My personal peace is knowing that I have been a devoted husband and loving father to my wife, Donna, and my grown children, Dana and Lindsay."

John Goodman, Public relations / marketing executive

"Peace is calmness, stillness in time, breathing deeply
and experiencing the moment."

Kristin Balko, Mother, wife, real estate agent

"Canoeing at sunset on a still northern lake punctuated by the moon's haunting call, one feels peace, serenity and comfort in the unfolding night."

John Suitor, Headmaster, Aspen Country Day School

"Peace is an individual, a group, and a country recognizing that there are no absolute positions of right and wrong. Peace is the ability to respect different views and engage and negotiate with those views.

"Peace is focusing on others' needs and concerns rather than one's own needs and concerns."

Judi Whetstine, Retired federal prosecutor. Currently consultant to an environmental law advocacy group and ombudsman.

"I am blessed to live in a place of beauty and peace. For me, peace is knowing I can send my children out the door without much worry.

"It is a reflection of nature and understanding that we are not in control.

"Peace is nurturing the simplicity of life and enjoying moments in time with no rules, conditions or judgments.

"The mountains are my place for peace, and for that I am grateful."

Kari Kiker, Massage therapist

"Peace comes from a sense of calm you experience when you live without fear."

Juliet E. Shield-Taylor, Mother, author, entrepreneur

"I feel peace when my students are being creative and learning. I feel peaceful as I watch them brainstorm and write about peace."

Katie Schwartz, Second grade teacher

"Peace is feeling, experiencing and expressing unconditional love in all aspects of your life: personal, private and professional. And of course, especially with your family."

Kristen Ruth Silberman, Mother, daughter, partner and realtor

"Peace comes to me in those moments of reflection when I can take the time to listen to the small, still voice within—and know I am at one with 'The Divine'."

Laurie Sue Brockway, Interfaith minister, author, and love coach

"Peace can be different things to different people. As a mother, peace is a day when the kids don't fight. As a wife, peace is a day of agreement, or at least for compromise and the knowledge that you are half of a whole. As a daughter, peace is acceptance of your parents' shortcomings and the realization of the wonder of them. Many of these things are actually about love.

"To me, there can be no peace without love. If we all take the time to find the good in each other and learn to love each other, we will all find peace."

Liz Scholer, Technology coordinator at an elementary school

"Peace is recognition that your neighbor has the same needs for love and security as yourself. It's the mind willing to be open to compromise born on love and knowledge. It's a desire for a calm and enduring respect for all inhabitants of our planet."

Lewis Katz, Businessman

"Peace is light. Peace is yourself. Peace is warmth. Peace is good. Peace is love. Peace is music. Peace is friendship. Peace is forgiveness. Peace is sharing with each other. Peace is cooperation with each other."

Liam Rio

"Peace is a state of harmony with the universe being in harmony, being free of all worries—those resulting from past events, from present circumstances and even those we create from outcomes we have not witnessed yet. To be in peace one has to be in the constant awareness that everything happens for the highest good. That which we once desired may not be what brings us happiness.

"When we are in peace we learn to trust our instinct. To be able to trust our instinct one must be aware that we are all connected to each other and to a higher being that is pure love and peace. Yes, we are surrounded by a world full of disturbances, but we can resurface that state of peacefulness by reconnecting to its higher source and constantly remembering that we were made to his likeness. If we were made to his likeness, then peace must be within us all."

Linnette Padilla, Spiritual Practice, BK yogi, Raya yo meditation

"His wellspring of grace blesses us with peace and joy."

"For Jesus said, 'Peace I leave with you. My peace I give you. I do not give to you as the world gives. Do not let your hearts be troubled and do not be afraid'."

Kristina Hurrell-Krakovitz, Owner of SpaFari; global
fitness adventures, spiritual journeys, wildlife eco-tours

"When I was a kid, as I blew out the candles on my birthday cake each year, I always wished for world peace—no more war. 'Let everyone be happy, and let no one be sad.'

"I thought that if these birthday wishes really did come true, then how could I possibly waste it on myself and not go for the really big one…world peace! I guess my desire was for no conflict between friends, family, countries. I still make that exact same wish every year. A childhood mantra that still plays in my mind.

"Back then peace to me meant the absence of war. The absence of cruelty. As a young child of the sixties, I truly felt life was unfair for so many and that peace between races, countries was all that we needed. Now that I am much older, the desire for peace has become much more personal. My adult mantra is to be blissfully content with life as it is in this moment. To be able to find peace in living each day, in enjoying the journey and not just waiting to reach a destination.

"To find peace in being a mom and a wife, when I have moments of frustration with my children or my husband, to remember how blessed I am to have them in my life.

"Peace to me is looking at life the way it is and finding the beauty in that and not in the way we wish it would be. If we could all do that maybe my childhood wish for world peace would come a little closer to becoming reality. When we all find peace within ourselves the whole world feels the benefit."

Lysa Usher Reed, Mom and actress

"Peace is love. Without love there is no peace."

Lynnette Schindler, Daughter, sister, wife, mother and grandmother

⚭

"Peace can mean many things. Knowing one's self, accepting who you are and saying 'I'm okay.' That's peace.

"Living in a world where we respect differences and try to understand other cultures would certainly promote peace.

"Living in a world where there are no worries, no natural disasters, no greed and only love. That's peace."

Marcie Chaiken, Retired

⚭

"To me, an interesting concept of world peace would be if everyone obeyed the Golden Rule 'Do unto others as you would have others do unto you.' It would mean never having to look over your shoulder in life. Because peace is a place where anguish and hatred do not exist.

"I am convinced that in every human being there's a longing for peace and serenity. At this moment in time we could use all the peace we can get."

Lorri Bleiweiss, Mother of four and jewelry designer

"Peace is what I find when I remember to come from a place of love."

Lisa Kane Jung, Health services and media production

"As long as we have been thinking primates, walking the plains of East Africa some 3.5 million years ago, we have waged war against other families, tribes, nations, races, and civilizations. At times, we have even accepted a temporary cessation of war. But we have never experienced true peace because through it all we have both consciously and unconsciously also waged a relentless war on our planet and *all* the species that inhabit it.

"Our war on nature is one we cannot win — a war we must not win. Were we to conquer so too will we be humbled. Were we to seek surrender we would have only succeeded in capturing ourselves. Ultimately our war on nature is a war on all that sustains us, provides for us, protects and nurtures us — it is a war with ourselves.

"Thus the defeat of nature is the defeat of humans.

"Peace thus is less about the absence of violence against humans but the absence of violence against humanity itself."

M. Sanjayan, Lead scientist, The Nature Conservancy

"Peace must first live within our minds, hearts and homes before it can go out to live in the world."

Marco Borges, Personal trainer

🐇

"Going to sleep at night without a worry on my mind."

Marilyn Borges, Wife and mother

🐇

"Peace is something that every human being searches for in the depth of his own heart.

"Peace is love and love is peace.

"When man conquers the meaning of peace then there will be peace on earth."

Maria Pia Buccellati, Designer

🐇

"Peace is harmony."

Mark Cann, CEO of charity and business

🐇

"Awakening – divine love or peace is the only way – to reconcile and heal. It's our Divine heritage; the flowering and the awakening to grace itself , ,if we're only open to it.

"Our family was fortunate to have our parents, Laura and Mickey They consciously tried to live from their hearts. They both knew that there was much the mind couldn't solve. They always reminded us what love meant, and that it was more important than who was right or who was wrong. If we shift to that state of consciousness where we no longer see a problem, but see instead the sacredness of life, we will find peace. The heart knows that all souls are sacred.

"We must give up conflict and go into the silence, that sacred space, and live from our heart center. Only then can we bring about peace to ourselves, our loved ones, and the world."

Lonna Brockway, Property manager

"The word 'peace' initially puts a smile on any face. It causes me to stop and reflect about the 60's—the period by which I was coming of age. Two fingers in the air, faded blue jeans, tie-dye, Woodstock, free love; these are just a few signs that there was more of an easy collective consciousness back then.

"Today, the word peace seems daunting; it evokes the feeling that it would take a great deal of effort and energy, and it would all be to no avail.

"Peace seems like war. Everyone has a different agenda in order to effect peace. I feel communication is the key. The high tech world seems to fragment the collective consciousness. Therefore, in order to change the world, one must take the responsibility personally and visualize what peace would feel like; what would make you feel better. And then that smile will come easily once again."

Marsha Klein, Wife, mother, artist

⚬

"The Navajo tribe of Indians have a word: *Hozho*. It loosely translates as harmony.

"A view of the world that allows for all things to have their unique function in nature. And to be in some sort of cooperation and symbiosis with each other.

"Is this peace? Probably. Is this possible? I doubt it."

Marvin Chaiken, Retired

"At first glance peace can seem bland and dull; the absence of violence, a lack of conflict, no war. Yet when we examine peace we find it's not that at all.

"Peace is a state of being, an action and a result. It begins in our hearts, drawing from some mysterious inexhaustible source that becomes available regardless of the circumstances whenever we choose to sweep away the landmines of resentment, fear, suspicion, anger, mistrust, greed and envy. –

"Peace is the assurance that all is well and all will be well. Peace requires great wisdom, faith, strength and courage. The presence of peace causes surety, serenity, confidence, trust, and healing.

"Peace is the deep sense of satisfaction that must have been experienced when God created the world and pronounced it good. Peace is how God would be and what God would do moment by moment everywhere in every situation, right now and always."

Mary Pat Brennan, Women's Program Coordinator for Washington National Cathedral Center for Global Justice and Reconciliation

"When two or more parties enter into an agreement and live up to that agreement, this is peace. It's all right to agree and disagree; however, if one party wishes to change all or part of an agreement then all parties must enter into renegotiation and also agree to modifications or uphold the original agreement.

"Part of an agreement shouldn't include clauses such as: If one party does not live-up to all or part of said agreement—the other party may 'blow-up' the other party. This would not be peace.

"Neither 'freedom fighters' nor 'terrorists' are peace keepers. The 'good guys' must use the threat of withholding peace to keep the 'bad guys' at bay.

"What is bad? 'Live and let live' is a better motto than 'live and let die.' Peace will never be an easy goal to achieve and maintain.

"Peace is not a four-letter word. Kill is a four-letter word."

Michael Buysse, Businessman

"Peace is knowing that regardless of what may happen to me, my family, my country or world, God is in control and will do what is in the best interest for 'His' people.

"Peace is knowing that with God, nothing is impossible.

"Can I hear an 'Amen'?"

Myra O'Brien, Homemaker and husband's administrator

"Peace for me begins with having the understanding that I am in control of my actions and that I can make the choices each day to guide my children from a place of love and respect. To truly listen more than speak. And to treat those around me with kindness.

"Allowing God to take on the direction of my choices and the burden of the outcome brings me inner confidence and serenity. Philippians 4:6: 'Be anxious for nothing, but in everything by prayer and supplication with thanksgiving let your requests be made known to God.' True Peace!"

Michelle Hocknell, Figure skating coach

"Peace is both an inner state of tranquility and acceptance, as well as a state of non-conflict among societies. In theory, one could have inner peace while engaged in social conflict.

"To an artist, peace may be satisfaction with one's philosophy and achievements, pride in one's life, and optimism regarding the future—all leading to the lack of turmoil.

"Peace in all respects is what mankind best strives for. Advocacy for any cause should be pursued with a sense and goal of peace.

"Peace is utopian and conscious. It's love and understanding. Peace is good."

Nelson Shanks, Artist, teacher

"Peace comes from within. It's an internal sense of calm. Peace is our birthright and in our busy lives, we sometimes forget. In the quiet stillness and beauty of nature we can truly connect with the peace in our hearts.

"It's a challenge to find that peace in the midst of our stressful daily lives. To find and create peace in ourselves when there is chaos around us takes daily practice. To be peaceful in the midst of a crisis is a challenge. Chanting by monks, beautiful music, and pure love can connect us to the inner peace that we all deserve in our life.

"Sometimes feeling peace can be as simple as petting your dog, a child's innocent smile, the sound of an ocean, or a beautiful sunset. We are blessed in our life with all these gifts to help us remember that peace is our birthright."

Millinda Sinnreich, Registered nurse involved in holistic medicine and nutrition

"Peace is having enough confidence in oneself to be able to accept the differences of others."

Peggy Scharlin Ben-Hamoo, Mother and real estate agent

"To me, the obvious technical definition of peace is the avoidance of conflict, whether you're talking about relationships with other nations or other people, family and friends, or yourself.

"There's a broader meaning, particularly in the context of dealing with others or in evaluating yourself. This broader context means that you're satisfied with the relationship. If you're at peace with yourself, then you're satisfied with your life, and the way things are going. Perhaps in a more negative way, you're resigned to the situation. If you're at peace with your family and friends, or if you're not struggling, you can accept things as they are without being upset.

"Another concept of peace is 'give me some peace and quiet.' A relaxing time when you're not being harassed by other things; a period of relaxation and enjoying things as they are. 'Peace' is also a greeting – wishing someone 'peace'.

"I'm not a philosopher nor have I looked in a dictionary to come up with my definitions – just my own thoughts."

Neil G. Bluhm, Real estate and investments

"Peace is relative in all its forms. It resonates to all mankind's heart, body, mind and soul individually.

"Peace for me is the serene feeling of oneness with the omnipotent and living God. It's extolling the goodness of God, reaching out for his divine Love, and thanking God daily for the living breath that he has given me as gift of life.

"Peace is the calmness of the mind, attuned only to that which is 'beautiful and perfect,' in the quietude of prayers, a fulfilled sense of tranquility, harmony and joy, devoid of all forms of selfishness. It is the shining glory of the purity of the soul.

"Is world peace attainable? In today's trivial and turbulent times, the vicissitudes of life that beset mankind is beyond the ordinary. It vacillates into the far reaches of the universe crying out, wailing for peace.

"Peace is elusive. On God's easel of Divine perfection, bleak shadows on the nature of man blurs the magnificent spectrum of colors and shades. God's almighty and powerful hand alone can gather and mold it together into 'One Global Whole.'

"Only when the venoms of the earth are crushed into smithereens and thrown into the dark abyss of God's ocean of wrath, never to rise up again, then and only then will infinite peace emerge triumphant and resonating to the four corners of the earth deeply touching the hearts and minds of mankind.

"Only then will the soft, uplifting music of the sphere waft in the spirit of everlasting 'Harmony and Joy,' and the blessed words 'Peace Be With You,' will infinitely bear its true and Godly meaning."

Nelia G. Alewine, Wife and retried business owner

"The Hebrew word for peace is *Shalom*. Every Hebrew word has a three-letter root, and in this case it's SH-L-M, which means 'wholeness' or 'completeness.' Therefore, one who feels complete or whole is at peace.

"This sense of completion is also the highest mystical attainment. Oneness with G-d is completeness. Oneness with one's world is peace. Oneness with one's partner is an esoteric path to completeness, to peace. William Blake wrote, 'The worm forgives the plow that cuts it.' That is completeness. That is unshakeable peace.

"On the other hand, a sense of lack or imbalance is the opposite of peace. One who needs something, one who feels aggrieved, one who feels empty inside, does not know peace. This is interminable restlessness."

Nathan Katz, Ph.D., Professor of Religious Studies and Director, Center for the Study of Spirituality, Florida International University

"Peace isn't the absence of conflict. Peace is learning how to navigate conflict without resorting to violence."

Rabbi Rami Shapiro

"War is costly. Peace is priceless."

Anonymous

"For me there are two kinds of peace.

"The first is inner peace: a sense of quiet, tranquility, contentment and balance. It's the way I feel sitting on my patio, watching the palm trees blowing in the breeze and the ducks floating on the lake. When I sit on a beach watching the water lap at the sand, or hearing the laughter of a child who has just touched the ocean for the first time.

"The second is outer peace. A desire to see a world without hate, prejudice, envy, jealousy or fear. A world in which one could travel anywhere without fear. A world without conflicts or wars. Just think how nice it would be to turn on the evening news and hear happy things!"

Randy H. Schenkman, Physician

"Four months ago I watched my mother die. She was in relatively good health except for congestive heart failure, which slowly caused her 93-year-old body to shut down over a period of a couple years. She remained lucid and coherent, and she laughed and joked in her typical child-like manner up to just two days before her death. While she lay unconscious, perfectly still as her breaths gradually became more and more shallow, my niece, my brother, and I sat in her room those last days, keeping company and keeping vigil. You might think that where I'm heading with this would be something about her peaceful countenance or her finally coming to peace, but that isn't it.

"You see, if anyone might have lived a life with a unique perspective on peace it was my mother. She was blind and deaf from around the age 10. She had a rare but not unknown condition called Usher's Syndrome. Eighty-three years is a long time to live in such a physically limiting world. But my mother was one of the most Pollyanna-like personalities I've ever known. She spread joy and attracted love wherever she went—especially those last 15 or so years when she lived in retirement care facilities. It was one of her many rare gifts.

"As we watched her those last days of shallow breaths, and knew that last breath was soon inevitable, and when I watched her take that final breath, lying totally still and without pain, it was undeniably clear to me that it was nothing more than the cessation of the happy but tired 93-year-old body. My mother was and is clearly still there and the imprinted image of her body and her living spirit remain vivid and ineradicable in my mind's eye.

"When I think of peace, I think of that image of my mother's last breath. And when I think of my mother's living spirit, I feel peace."

Orion Pitts, Spiritual seeker, office administrator, church musician

"Peace is the final and most noble gift God gave to his creatures after a life of devotion and pure love.

"Peace is the most precious flower that can grow and survive with the seed of love in the human garden.

"Peace is the only anesthesia to endure the extrication of hate and greed during life.

"Peace is the hidden diamond in the unpredictable darkness of the human brain."

Renato Taverna, Maitre D'

"The word for peace in Hebrew is *Shalom,* which comes from the root meaning wholeness. There can be no peace if I am feeling separate, or if there are parts of myself that I have rejected.

"Peace requires that I connect myself to all of life and also, that I reclaim parts of myself that have been hidden away.

"To heal the feelings of separation and alienation I begin by suspending judgment and opening up my heart to the possibility of compassion, first for myself and then for others. Peace comes to me with the glimpse that my miniscule part is also integral to the whole of life.

"The road to peace is also the path of self-awareness, and self-acceptance. Whatever remains hidden inside myself will be projected out on someone else, and they will become my enemy. Peace comes to me when I accept that I am in process, that even my mistakes are holy. Peace comes to me when I know that we are all in this together. Then our wrestling can become a dance. Everyone and everything becomes my teacher. And each moment becomes an opportunity to come home."

Rabbi Shefa Gold, Runs retreats and teaches in communities throughout the world

"Peace is accepting yourself and others – just as they are."

Paula Johnson, Mediator

"I believe we are all in search of complete and total peace, which can never really be reached.

"It requires us to be at peace with others and at peace with ourselves. To have peace of mind is to be content with life, body and mind. Peace in one's life can be so fragile and vulnerable and at times so solid the rest.

"Everyone has something they enjoy doing. For some, it might be exercising, golfing, or fishing. Some find peace in looking at their children play and others in watching a beautiful view of the sun setting over the ocean. It brings us joy and peace: a time when all your worries are lifted and taken away.

"One must have at least one person who makes us happy and brings peace to our lives.

"During these difficult times, one will question if there is peace in our lives and in the world. But peace isn't something we can measure. We have to be at peace with ourselves, bring peace and joy to those around us, and hope that it's contagious.

"I tell my good friends that to be at peace is to live without regrets.

"If we could see peace for just one day, it would be difficult not to want it every day."

Ralph Yara, Computer consultant

"I think of peace as the love and good feelings that we give others. Peace is an inner feeling from the heart. God promises us that when we have problems he will help us deal with them and give us inner peace if we have faith.

"Sometimes when I am troubled or feel depressed, my grandson's visit seems to melt away all my problems. I have such a peaceful feeling being with him.

"My greatest inner peace comes from knowing that when our journey here is done, God has better plans prepared for us eternally. This inspires me to strive each day to be a better person.

"Let's pray each day for world peace and good will toward men."

Patsy King, Retired school cafeteria worker

"Peace is the mother's sigh when she hears her baby's first cry.
Peace is the loved one's sigh when the last breath is witnessed.
Inspire in Spirit
Expire gone to Spirit
Peace."

Rita E. Marsh, Author of programs in mind, body
and spirit integration; established The Davi Nikent Center
for the Human Flourishing

"In general, outside of geography and politics, one might say peace is 'the absence of...' One reaches a state when there is the absence of: unworthiness, jealousy, anger, pride, indifference, ego, self-indulgence lack of awareness, intent, worldly desire, abuse of power, desire to be right, attachment, blame, fear, guilt, indecision, judgment, reaction, revenge, and shame.

"I believe peace, true peace, is a matter of balance. It's a constantly shifting state because each moment the universe is different. The more awareness one has, the more one is able to be at one with the universe. That oneness is peace. It is also love.

"Peace begins inside one's own self, when anger, hate and unworthiness is weeded out. The more these negative aspects are weeded out, the more room there is for awareness, gratitude, courage, and compassion—the positive aspects of your self. The more positive aspects you have, the more you can give to others, are able to see another person's sameness to you, and cherish the differences between you. Once we are cherishing differences and aware of sameness, then it's so very hard to feel violence or hatred toward others. Then we slip into the land of "the absence of...'

Richard Scalzo, Caretaker and chela

꽃

"Peace is not being hurried."

Carman Luntzel, Restaurateur

"Peace is a unified self, a state of mind of living in the present; the absence of internal conflict; the acceptance of who you are without comparison to others; the realization that there are things you can't change or control; the acceptance of imperfections. If you have these basic tenets as part of your life, you'll know what brings you peace.

"Peace is defined differently for each person. It could simply be watching your grandchildren laugh, seeing your dog sleep in the sun, or walking on a beach."

Sanford L. Fox, Former CEO, executive recruiting firm

"Peace is unconditional love, surrender, beyond truce, or condition. Spiritual evolution is experienced by the universal progression of peace, characterized by increasing personal freedom. It's derived from the accumulated experience of mankind, and from the teachings of many masters, including Jesus, The Prince of Peace."

Robert Mandich, Architect

"If some of these thoughts might still be of value, I'd like to share them with you:

"Peace is knowing how to love.

"Make peace with yourself first. It'll become a powerful force that will resonate with others.

"Formula for peace: love and hate. Good and bad. Black and white. Happy and sad. Weakness and strength. They are each singular elements which humankind experiences at both ends of the spectrum. Peace is the point in the center of these extremes.

"Understand that our universe cannot function without an appropriate balance of positive and negative forces at the atomic and molecular level. Become aware that this universal law permeates all.

"Dedicate your life to always finding harmonious balance between opposing forces, rather than repel one or the other. Then you shall have the formula for peace."

Robert Doornick, International Robotics, Inc.

"When all units work together in harmony, towards a common goal, that is peace.

"Of course one may ask, what is a unit? A unit can be cell in the human body or an atom in matter. Perhaps a unit is a space ship or a continent. A unit is an entity of nature. When that entity works in harmony with other entities, peace has been achieved."

Russ Ousis, Broadcasting entrepreneur

"Peace is tranquility in your heart.
Freedom of expression.
Harmony in the world."

Ruth Ann Marshall, Retired president of
Americas MasterCard Worldwide

"Peace for me is the personal relationship with Jesus Christ. I have peace in knowing that I am his child and that when I breathe my last breath I will be with Him in glory—for all of eternity. My hope comes from promises made in God's word, the Bible.

"There isn't a shadow of a doubt that heaven, in God's presence, is my eternal destiny. "

Ruth Babbitt, High school teacher and church secretary

"Let there be peace on earth and let it begin with me. It is a phrase often heard in church.

"Peace to me begins from within and originates from being confident and comfortable with myself. It allows me to be open with diverse views, beliefs and religions."

Sally Stetson, Business owner

"Peace is complete harmony. In harmony with the people you surround yourself with. Harmony between nations. Peace involves being respectful and having empathy for others. Peace starts with oneself. Only someone who is at peace with himself can be at peace with others. Peace of mind allows one to live in peace with others and surroundings."

Sandra Fiorenza, Full time mother, entrepreneur, and real estate broker

"Peace is having positive thoughts about myself and others."

Sarah Gabsi

"Peace is getting in touch with the tranquility and quietness within ourselves. This consciousness radiates out to the world with infinite possibilities."

Sharon Hills-Bonczyk, Manager of Family Services, Children's Hospital and Clinics, Minneapolis and St. Paul, Minnesota

"Peace to me is not hearing the sound of gun shots, not hearing about soldiers dying, and going outside of your door and saying hello to your neighbors."

Shlomo Ben-Hamoo, Restaurateur, real estate, father

"Peace is your original religion."

Sister Jenna, Spiritual mentor, writer, activist, director, Brahma Kumaris, Washington D.C.

"Peace is the opposite of worry. It's knowing that I can give all of my burdens to the Lord to handle, and having faith that all is well with Him in control. Wherever Jesus reigns, there is peace where there was once hopelessness. When he is Lord of my life, there is peace in my life. Peace does not mean to be in a place where there is no noise, trouble, or hard work. Peace means to be in the midst of all those things and still be calm in your heart. That is the real meaning of peace."

The Peace Prayer of St. Francis

Lord, make me an instrument of your peace;
Where there is hatred, let me sow love;
When there is injury, pardon;
Where there is doubt, faith;
Where there is despair, hope;
Where there is darkness, light;
And where there is sadness, joy.
Grant that I may not so much seek
To be consoled as to console;
To be understood, as to understand,
To be loved as to love;
For it is in giving that we receive,
It is in pardoning that we are pardoned,
And it is in dying that we are born to eternal life.

Sher Foster, Artist, Executive Director, Crisis Hotline; art teacher

"Peace is a place where a child can play, think and be happy without being afraid.

"Peace, as a parent, is watching my children play uninterrupted by the outside world.

"Peace is a place where hate isn't tolerated."

Stacey Greene, Busy mother

"Peace is the sunlight of the spirit."

Sunny Scribante, Presidential appointee

"Peace resides within the heart. It is born of the knowledge that we are truly loved and provided for. Peace is the blossom which comes from the seed of Divine unconditional love."

Susan Pierce, Environmental consultant and mother

"Peace is the atmosphere of acceptance, love and understanding. It's a place of the mind where it is safe. Peace is the ultimate luxury that we are entitled to have. Peace is a real place; our true destiny."

Steve Guttenberg, Actor

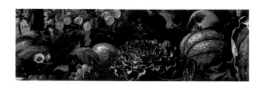

"During Roman times, the concept emerged that peace, or pax, can only result from a successful war. In the modern world, peace is generally thought of as the absence of hostility, conflict, war, or disagreement. It can also be a state of mind, in which tranquility, calm, and serenity are the hallmarks of a harmonious state of being.

"Is peace an optimal state for human endeavors? Many of the most successful politicians had careers that blossomed during wartime: George Washington, Abraham Lincoln, Franklin Roosevelt, Winston Churchill, Harry Truman, and Dwight Eisenhower had careers that benefited from armed conflict. Of course, war can also be a disaster for politicians. Let me turn to science about which I am more of an expert.

"The peaceful pursuit of science is not generally the most productive. Major steps in science occur in the midst of intellectual conflict. Opposing points of view intersect and experimental data accumulate to answer the questions that have pitted groups of scientists against each other. The mental hostility can become severe. Unlike war, physical hostility is not deployed, but the anger can be extreme.

"A bellwether for the emergence of a major advancement in science is the depth of feeling that the various protagonists and antagonists project in their heated arguments about what is true and what is false. Winston Churchill is attributed to have said, 'In science, you do not need to be polite, you only need to be right.'

"What is wonderful about scientific conflict is that data are the final arbiters. The experimental data define a natural phenomenon; as a verifiable truth emerges, the battles subside. When a new scientific truth has been established through a rigorous process, a peaceful consensus replaces the conflict. Notably, the fruits of past conflict—original ideas, fresh perspectives, new paradigms—can be harvested in a period of relative tranquility, or peace.

"So do scientists want to live in peace? Yes, they are generally against war because they understand the horrors that modern weaponry brings. A few scientists are exceptionally lucky because their research creates a conflict from which a fundamental discovery emerges. Scientific conflict was certainly an important aspect of my own career.

"We all seek a calm and serene world, desire harmony, and yearn for an absence of disagreement. However, the peaceful world may not be optimal for all endeavors. Most of the transformative events in the history of our planet have not emerged by peaceful, tranquil transitions. Surprisingly, periods of conflict can spur great advances, particularly in science and medicine, some of which substantially improve our planet.

"I thank Panos Philandrinos for his excellent research on the etymology of the word 'peace'."

Stanley B. Prusiner, Nobel Prize-winning neurologist

"Societal peace ensures survival for the group, and depends on cooperation. Optimal personal survival and peace depends on selfish choices of living with productive people, eating a diet that nurtures an efficient biochemistry as well as staying in nature and receiving the rhythmic calming energy of the sun's rays.

"The reward of peaceful feeling, contentment, and pain relief within the individual are created when an electrical circuit is completed in one's brain by a simple chain of four protein amino acids filling the appropriate receptor site. This uplifting motivating internal morphine-like opiate is called an endorphin.

"Endorphins are programmed to be released when we breathe deeply, pray, sing, chant, laugh, please our parents, help others, are praised, fill our stomach, empty our bowels, hug, have sex, stretch, exercise, are stressed or experience pain. This peaceful pain-relieving signal of contentment ensures healthy bodily rhythm as well as survival in the hunter-gatherer lifestyle.

"Toxicity accumulates from people settling in one place. It's compounded by weak soils, storage, processing, preservation and cooking. Toxicity and excess leads to irritability, righteous anger and confrontational mood swings. Perceived scarcity and selfish addictions lead to the opposites of peace, strife and war.

"Enlightened altruistic selflessness promotes the most rewarding individual long-term survival strategy."

Steven N. Green, Holistic dentist

"Peace is a power that supports the deepest laughter and the most far-reaching connections. Peace makes us safe and frees our heart to celebrate life. It lets us love our neighbor and stills the agony of those who call us their foe. Peace is a power that turns weapons to rusting relics.

"Peace is a mighty power. Like a frictionless superconductor, it powers our greatest achievements, effortlessly, without bound. Peace is a uniting force.

"When our body hears the harmony of the universe's multidimensional orchestra, we transcend time and space, becoming 'the peace that passeth understanding'."

Tanai Starrs, Visionary, co-founder of The Mastery of the Heart School, biochemist and multidimensional scientist

"Peace to me is the fulfillment of dreams. My lifelong dream was to have a husband and beautiful healthy children. I was lucky enough to have a wonderful girl and boy. Peace to me is also having two healthy parents."

Tara Elias Schuchts, Realtor, homemaker

"Imagine a dove gracefully flying through the vast skies with purity and innocence. So unassuming. So completely unaware of what message it brings forth. What you see in the eyes and the heart of that dove is peace

"For peace to happen is to be involved, yet uninvolved. To be free from the burden of knowing. Free from opinions. Free from directing.

"True peace lies behind a mind that is still. A mind that has no ripple, no movement of thoughts. A mind that is focused and concentrated. Behind such a mind lies the heart of who we are. Behind such a mind is the 'essence' of peace.

"Peace is loyal. It never leaves us. It never wavers, nor diminishes. It exists for all time. We forget that it is there. But, when we turn within and catch a glimmer of it, the heart jumps for joy. We find after so long that which we thought was lost. And then when there is peace, I am afraid of nothing. I can smile. I am kind.

"The courage, the smile and kindness that is born of peace is such that it reaches all the world, like a gentle touch upon the shoulder. It heals and brings to life those who had lost hope. It works magically and invisibly. And those who are touched by it know not from where it comes, but they surely know that it has come

"Those who are touched by this peace are able to share that peace with others. And so it comes to pass that there is the fragrance of peace in all our world."

Suman Kalra, Voluntary worker, Brahma Kumaris, UK

"Peace is not merely the absence of conflict, but creation restored to the wholeness, health, and balance God intended. In Hebrew this word is 'Shalom', in Arabic 'Salaam'. Ironically, the name 'Jerusalem' means 'God's Peace', and yet the city has known nothing but conflict for centuries. But the name itself holds up the hope and vision that God intends God's creation to be in complete harmony with itself and with God "

The Reverend Wilfred Allen Faiella, Episcopal priest; rector, St. Stephen's Episcopal Church, Coconut Grove, Florida

"Personally, I would answer the question: Not to achieve some pithy intellectual answer, but to sit in stillness long enough to have a direct personal experience in the present moment.

"Are peace, joy and contentment already here? Is that our natural state? Where did we go and why are we missing it? Asking the question brings us into a deeper inquiry of the present moment. Simply to stop arguing with what is already here, reality, brings us back to God. Fearless simplicity."

Todd Welden, Medical anthropologist

🍂

"Peace is completely knowing yourself and your limits and then being completely satisfied. It's being happy when you get up in the morning, and happy when you go to bed at night.

"Peace is always being with your family, never having to look behind for what you have done in the past.

"Peace is always looking forward to tomorrow, and wishing the world was at peace."

Tom Hassert, Jr., Car dealer

🍂

"Peace, I believe, is only perceived in the eye of the beholder.
It can be perceived in very communal or personal terms. For someone in a war torn country, peace can be the cessation of armed conflict. For someone who lives with daily gang or drug violence in a neighborhood, peace can mean going to sleep without hearing gunfire at night or sending a child to school without fear or worry that harm will come his or her way.

For someone who has lost a close family member, peace may be found in the solitude of one's memories. And for others peace may be as near as the tranquility and feeling of being at peace when sitting on the dock of the bay or bank of a river on a beautiful day."

Tom Sprague, Attorney

"Peace is the silence in which we hear not the sounds of war, nor the anguish of the pain and suffering left in its wake.

"Peace is the silence in which we hear not the cries of hunger, or racism, or civil disturbance, nor even a disquieting or oppressive thought.

"In the silence, spirit rises. There is no 'friend or foe,' no 'rich or poor', no 'us and them.' Only Advaita. 'Not two.' Thus, there is only One."

Tony Tognucci, Teacher of Eastern philosophy and Eastern health modalities

"Peace is being surrounded by the beauty of nature and all of God's creations. And knowing that His spirit and all of those I love are always with me."

Trudy Holderby, Retired customer service representative, 1975 Miss Washington-World

"Peace is the pure oxygen that helps sustain our life, the clean water which nourishes our growth.

"It's the best clothing keeping us warm in the Siberian cold. And the Golden Bridge that connects the whole world.

"Peace is the diamond that beautifies our body and the poetry that delights our voice; the meditation that soothes our mind, and the antidote that heals our ailments.

"Peace is the best friend who never turns unfriendly or foe. The greatest master who always instructs positively. The leader who is appreciated by diversities.

"Peace is the strong handshake we give; the warm arms with which we embrace every human; the good heart with which we respect others.

"Peace is the jumbo tree that bears sweet fruits; the evergreen plant which blooms stunning flowers; the nectar that enriches our positive energy. And the lotus which is free from contaminations.

"Peace is cool as His Holiness the Dalai Lama. It's clean air. A big smile like a full moon.

"Peace is worth cherishing—like brilliant eyes.

"Peace. *She-de. Santi.*"

Ven Jampa Tenzin, Drepung Loseling Phukhang

"Peace is harmony between beings. In the animal kingdom, peace is related to survival rules. As humans we can practice ways of reaching that harmony only if we want to have a better life in terms of humanity beyond ego. Only if we accomplish peace for humanity we will have peace for ourselves.

"By being more compassionate and respectful, we can find harmony even when we don't agree with something or somebody. We will reach peace through harmony only when we practice compassion and respect."

Veronica Fazzio, Art teacher and contemporary visual artist working in mixed media, installations, video and sculptures

"Peace is a state of mind. It's happiness with yourself and the surroundings in which you live."

Walter J. Ganzi Jr., Restaurateur, hotel owner and operator

"Loving. And being Loved."

Wayne Schuchts, Relationships and commercial real estate

"Peace is a word that all living beings look for and want in our lives. We are faced with temporary peace, but it is not enough. We need peace of mind.

"We can assume peace of mind when we are able to eliminate ignorance, jealousy, attachment and especially 'selfishness.'

"When selfishness is our master, we are unable to get peace of mind. For that, we have to be selfless and give to others. We must serve others before self. When you will accept the selfless, it will bring you permanent peace of mind."

Yeshi Jample, Buddhist monk

"Peace is the smell of my children, when I bend down to kiss them goodnight. The scent hits me straight in my chest and acts like a muscle relaxer and protective shield— all at once."

Yvonne Carey, Editor-in-chief, magazine publishing

"Peace cannot be kept by force. It can only be achieved by understanding."

Albert Einstein

"Peace is a nation's best security. Peace is too important to be left to politicians. If the people will lead, the leaders will follow."

Richard Goodwin, Chair, Board of Trustees,
Middle East Peace Dialogue Network, Inc.

"Discussions about peace have divided nations and families throughout the centuries. Think of our Civil War with brother fighting against brother or World War II where the perpetrator was genuinely evil. The cavalry and the Indians, Christian crusades, and now terrorism, centuries of unrest in the Middle East and threats of nuclear destruction. Will it ever end?

"I think of peace as politics and religion together--a personal and universal issue. If we could all find peace in our hearts to tolerate differences, forgive our enemies, help those in need and find refuge from selfishness then perhaps there would be hope for a better future.

"Remember John 14:27, 'Peace I leave with you; my peace I give unto you. Not as the world giveth, give I unto you. Let not your heart be troubled, neither let it be afraid.'"

Gayle Kenny Ray, Retired software consultant

"Personal peace is the soul's knowledge that life is being lived with honor, humility and compassion."

Rob Krakovitz, Holistic medical doctor

"Peace is the result of living our virtues…mindfully tapping into our qualities of joy, compassion and love every moment, every day.

"Peace is ignited by our generosity–of heart, of mind, of all who we are. When we give unconditionally out of love and pure intention, we open the spacious realm of peace – that perfect space which resides in each and every one of us."

Nancy Spears, CEO, genconnect.com, Author, *Buddha: 9 to 5.*

"Often in the early hours of morning, but not always.
Sometimes in the noon day, in the maddening rush,
when my thinking is attuned with my heart,
and the outward shouting and calling is deafened by
an inner voice. And I hear as if for the first time,
an old familiar sound, I am filled with Peace,
reassured that all is not lost, the circle is not broken."

Eric L. Motley

"Peace is love. My mom is peace. Peace fills the air. Peace is family."

Ayla Potamkin, age 9

"Peace means love and kindness. No harm or fighting. Peace also means calm, relaxed and respectfulness for all the virtues. Peace to the world! Peace is also eating healthy food."

Riley Ganzi, age 10

"Peace is meditating happy thoughts, love and kindness with strong energy. Peace is friends and family, never raising your voice, and always being kind."

Alura Potamkin, age 9

"For me, peace is acceptance. It's keeping my perceptions in check. Peace comes with gratitude and departs with wanting to have a nicer car, a bigger house, more vacation time, more money and more time with my son.

"It's wanting to change the way I look, the way my back goes out every time I stop doing yoga, the way the jerk in front of me is driving, the way people trash the planet and the way that they waste, waste, waste.

"The simple task of remembering all that I have—a healthy and wonderful family, when so many others do not; a job that takes care of us when so many people are starving and have no options for medical care.

"The fact that we have enough is all I need to bring my peace back to me. The challenging part is remembering to employ that simple practice when life's little situations try to steal it away."

Joy Rigel, Green home consultant

&

"Peace is knowing my children are safe."

Alan Potamkin, Dad

&

"Peace is the capacity for happiness; the relational capacity to live slowly; to be able to sense the implicit interdependence and harmony among all life. It is when we feel safe and are able to feel gratitude."

Diana Whitney, President, Corporation for Positive Change, author, *The Power of Appreciative Inquiry*

🕊️

"War is only a cowardly escape from the problems of peace."

Thomas Mann

🕊️

"If you want to make peace, you don't talk to your friends. You talk to your enemies."

Moshe Dayan

🕊️

"I find peace in contemplation.
While contemplating a beautiful piece of art,
While contemplating the ocean,
While contemplating the rain.

"Most of all, I find peace every night
While putting my son to sleep,
contemplating his beautiful face
so sweetly, so peacefully
that is peace to me."

Adriana de Moura, Art dealer, mother

AFTERWORD

"Peace is a state of mind that has the quality of remaining undisturbed even in the face of any form of harm or benefit being dispensed by others. It is a balanced state of mental attitudes gained from pacification of negative emotions within oneself. Through this an individual is able to enjoy happiness at both the physical and mental level. If an individual person has it, he or she then has peace."

Lobsang Yonten, Drepung Loseling Monastery, India, received primary education at Lugu Lake school in Tibet and then entered the Tharlam Monastery where he received training in reading, writing, ritual and chanting.

"Based on the understanding that all other beings are equally the same and are, just as myself, wishing for happiness and no suffering, if an individual person's mind settles in a relaxed manner then this may be called peace."

Lobsang Choephel, Monk

"Peace refers to total accomplishment over one's desires.

When one's desires are fulfilled, only then would one be able to settle one's mind in its natural state.

This state of peace of mind settled in its natural form is sought after by all –rich or poor. It is the ultimate goal of all sentient beings."

Geshe Wanden Tashi, completed Geshe Degree education at Drepung Loseling Monastery, India

"It is not impossible for an individual to cultivate both hatred and compassion at the same time, but whenever hatred arises compassion subsides and vice versa. This is natural. This tells us that every moment of cultivating compassion, no matter for how long it might be experienced, are moments of peace.

"In support of what has already been stated, Buddha has said, 'The nature of mind is clear and lucid. All stains are but adventitious.' He who has a peaceful state of mind also has a pure motivation, a wide perspective, loving-kindness, respect for others and for wherever he resides, and is able to enjoy peace. Just as the sunrays dispel darkness in all directions, he who has peace of mind is also able to share joy and happiness to all. This is my firm belief.

"In short, pacification of the three delusions is Peace. This can be brought through happiness rooted in compassion and loving-kindness."

Sonam Dorjee, Drepung Loseling Monastery, India

"Here are different views on what is peace.

"For some, peace refers to enjoyment of human rights and for others it is a state of non-violence.

"For some it is attaining military hegemony and enjoying nuclear power. However, I view peace as referring primarily to mental peace and happiness. For example, the generation of a visual perception of a thing depends upon meeting with an external object, and the visual perception alone does not have the power to think or contemplate. Contemplation upon what one sees visually would require a mental thought process acting as the primary cause.

"How we react to what we have seen defines whether we have experienced peace and happiness or delusion and suffering. For me, happiness is obtained from maintaining brotherhood and affection amongst each other. For this reason, let us seek peace and pray for peace in the line of what the great master Aryadeva, has said:

For as long as space endure,
And for as long as living beings remain,
Until then may I too abide
To dispel the misery of the world."

Gungbar Chusang Rinpoche, Geshe Lharampa degree; highest level of monastic degree in Gelug order of Tibetan Buddhism; resident Professor at Drepung Loseling Monastery in India

"Normally, there is no peace because our mind is overwhelmed with attachment towards some and hatred towards others due to the power of delusions and conceptual constructions we have cultivated upon us. This is the root of all problems even to the level of poor relationships between nations. Hence, the opposite of above i.e. pacification of negative emotions can only produce perfect peace. And this is peace in the real sense.

"Lack of perfect mental peace will mean only temporary physical pleasure but not perfect peace. Primarily speaking, it is mental peace that can bring a harmonious balance between physical and mental entities.

"It is through total pacification of mental delusions that a perfect state of mental peace is possible. It is through cultivation of mental peace and happiness. A perfect state of universal peace is possible.

"Peace is sought even by the tiniest of creatures. Therefore, it is extremely important that we all understand its preciousness and supreme qualities. Because of our lack of this understanding even though we seek peace and happiness we only experience suffering.

"The great master Shantideva has said:

> *Although wishing to be rid of misery.*
> *They run towards misery itself,*
> *Although wishing to have happiness,*
> *Like an enemy they ignorantly destroy it.*

"If that is the case, you might wonder what then constitutes peace?

"If one were able to abide in a state of joy without being drawn by the force of negative attitudes and conceptual constructions, but remain grounded by less desire and more contentment, then temporary peace would be achieved.

"Moreover, when one is able to experience a spontaneous sense of joy free of jealousy whenever one sees other sentient beings obtain happiness, particularly one who is deemed one's enemy, then this is an obvious sign of genuine peace that one is experiencing.

"In short, one gains genuine peace and happiness only through wishing others happiness. As Shantideva has said:

> All happiness of this world
> Comes from wishing happiness for others.
> All miseries of this world
> Comes from wishing happiness for self.

"This teaching should be well thought about. May there be peace."

Ngawang Jinpa, received education up to the fourth standard in Tibet. He then entered Songtsen Ling monastery and received trainings in monastic ritual and recitations. In 1998 he left Tibet and joined Drepung Loseling Monastery in India and studied elementary epistemology, science of mind, Pramana, Abhisamayalankara and Madhyamaka. He is currently a student of the second year Vinaya class.

"Every day we do things, we are things that have to do with peace. If we are aware of our life, our way of looking at things, we will know how to make peace right in the moment we are alive."

Thich Nhat Hanh

"You who want peace can find it only by complete forgiveness."

A Course in Miracles

Peace in Different Languages

Peace, Shalom, Paz, Paix Heiwa, Salam, Alaafia, Ashtee, Baké, chibanda, Diakatra, Echnahcaton, Filemu, Gunnammwey, Hau, Hmetho, Iri'ni, Kagis, Kalilintad, K'e, Khanhaghutyun, Kinuinak, Paqe, Lape Haitian, Layent, Lumana, Mabuhay, Maluhia, Melelilei, Melino, Miers, Mina, Muka-muka, Musango, Mutenden, Nabad-Da, Nanna Ayya, Nerane'I, Nimuhore, Nirudho, Nye, Olakamigenoka, Puci, Paco, Pax, Pingan, Pokoj, Pyong'hwa, Rahu, Rangima'arie, Rauha, Rerdamaian, Rukun, Santi, Sat Gaai Oh, Santipap, Saq, Shîte, Sholim, Siochain, Sith, Soksang, Solh Dari, Sonqo, Sulh, Taika, Tecocatu, Thayu, Tsumukikiatu, Tuktuquil usilal, Tutkiun, Udo, Vride, Waki Ijiwebis-I, Wetaskiwin, Wolakota, Wontokode, Wo'okeyeh.

Lexie Brockway Potamkin

Lexie Brockway Potamkin brings a diverse career and extensive world travel to her work as author of *What is Peace?* A human rights activist, counselor and minister, she spent many years working in the worlds of business, entertainment and media. A former Miss World USA, she hosted her own talk show and eventually became a public relations professional working for Golin Harris Public Relations, Gold Mills Inc. and Rogers and Cowan Public Relations. At the height of her business success, having founded and sold her own PR firm, she returned to school for her Master's Degree in Applied Psychology from the University of Santa Monica. Her ensuing counseling work inspired her to the next spiritual step, becoming an ordained minister.

She has traveled the world and over the past decade has been a guiding force and inspiration for many charitable organizations. In Philadelphia, she was President of Resources for Children's Health and a trustee for the International House. Her passion for human rights has led her to speak before the United Nations as Vice President of the International League for Human Rights, and work with the Dalai Lama and Tibetan Buddhist monks.

Lexie and her husband founded an elementary school in Florida called Fisher Island Day School.

Lexie is studying at The Spiritual Paths Institute, with respected teachers, contemplative wisdom and applied spirituality that combines intellect, heart, and spiritual practice. She lives in Colorado with her family, four dogs, two cats, and a few hamsters.

Anatoly Ivanov

Anatoly Ivanov's early childhood was spent in a Moscow orphanage. He studied at the Moscow Academy of Art, and worked as an illustrator for the Moscow Children's Literature Publishing House.

Although he and his family were considered materially successful by Soviet standards, his desire to be freed of the ideological chains in Russian society drove him to immigrate with his wife and daughter to the United States after traveling in Europe.

Since his arrival in 1979 he has been a leading innovator in the art world with his lush, painstakingly detailed artwork spanning the entire emotional gamut.

Ivanov's work blends imaginative fantasy with spiritual and humanistic overtones. His symbolic creations speak to the very soul of the spectator. An Ivanov painting, usually in tempera, is a melding of painstaking craftsmanship and vivid imagination. His all-seeing eye gives him the ability to produce lush metaphors, which result in a new reality on canvas.

He has illustrated two other books, *Ol' Jake's Lucky Day* and *The Pied Piper of Hamelin*. Kirkus, in a starred review, said: "Boldly color-

126

ful drawings…reflect the whole gamut of emotions, from the ugly expressions of anger and greed on the villagers' faces to the brilliant visions of a child's paradise evoked by the Piper's magic flute."

He lives with his family in New Jersey.

Index